D1232985

MICROSOFT®
POWERPOINT®
2010

Trademarks

Disclaimer

The QuickClicks Reference Guide series is dedicated to all of CareerTrack's devoted customers. Our customers' commitment to continuing education and professional development inspired the creation of the award-winning *Unlocking the Secrets* CD-ROM series and the *QuickClicks Reference Guide* series.

Thank you for your continued support!

Contents

Introduction

Congratulations on your purchase of QuickClicks: PowerPoint 2010. You have invested wisely in yourself and taken a step forward in your personal and professional development.

This reference guide is an important tool in your productivity toolbox. By effectively using the word processing functions within Microsoft PowerPoint, you will be able to maximize your efficiency. The tips in this reference guide are written for the user who has a basic understanding of word processing and at least one year of experience using other Microsoft Office applications.

Anatomy of a Tip

Each tip displays the tip title in the top left corner and the tip category in the top right, so you always know where you are and what you are learning. Each tip is written in plain English. Some tips will include a "What Microsoft Calls It" reference to help you perform more effective searches for additional feature capabilities in Microsoft's help system.

Each tip is assigned a difficulty value from one to four, with one circle representing the easiest tips and four circles representing the hardest.

Difficulty: ●○○○

All tips begin with a business scenario, identified as **PROBLEM**.

SOLUTION explains how the demonstrated feature might be used to solve the problem. A set of easy-to-understand instructions follows.

Letter callouts, **A**, point to important parts of the screen. The names of all selections and buttons are bolded and easy to find.

Extras Include the Following

Icon	Name	What It Means
	Bright Idea	Bright ideas provide additional information about Excel or the features in question.
	Hot Tip	Hot Tips share related functions and features, or additional features and uses of the task being demonstrated.
	Caution	Cautions draw attention to situations where you might find yourself tripped up by a particularly complicated operation, instances when making an incorrect choice will cause errors you will have to correct, or times when very similar options might be confusing.

There are two other bonuses that do not have miniature icons. They are displayed at the end of tips, where appropriate. These are:

Icon	Name	What It Means
	Options	Options represent places where there are two or more ways to accomplish a task or where two or more results might be obtained, depending on the choices you make. Options icons appear within the text, and all relevant choices are next to the icon.
	Quickest Click	Quickest Clicks indicate there is a faster way to accomplish the same task taught in the tip. Shortcuts like this, though, may leave out important steps that help you understand the feature. Therefore, each tip teaches the most complete method for accomplishing a task, and a Microsoft Quickest Click appears if there is a faster option.

At the bottom of each page, you will see either a Continue or a Stop icon. These icons indicate whether a tip continues on the next page or if it is complete.

Understanding PowerPoint 2010

Microsoft PowerPoint is a powerful presentation program that enables you to easily create, modify, and share presentations with an audience of 1 to 1000. PowerPoint 2010 is more powerful than previous versions because new features and a new interface have improved usability and efficiency. In particular, PowerPoint 2010 has introduced many customization features that make setting a personalized workflow within the program easy and extremely efficient. PowerPoint 2010 also introduced powerful new media editing features that allow you to trim audio or video and edit images without having to leave PowerPoint. New sharing features let you prepare your presentation for internet delivery.

PowerPoint users can produce simple presentations, such as photo albums and speaker outlines, as well as complex presentations, such as self-running shows, interactive games, and audio-visual enriched slide shows. PowerPoint 2010 interfaces with other Microsoft Office 2010 applications to create presentation materials (Word) and data feeds that automatically keep presentations up to date (Excel).

PowerPoint 2010 is a powerful tool for a variety of users:

Teachers or Trainers: Create educational materials for use in lectures (with a variety of options such as embedded media, animations, and presentation tools), in self-running kiosks (with a variety of options for creating interactive tasks), and in classroom management (with a variety of templates for classroom seating and more).

Students: Create presentations and handouts for reports that will be much more impressive than poster board.

Managers and Team Leads: Create detailed presentations to explain expectations or inform superiors of your success.

Small Business Owners: Create marketing materials, personalized customer reports, or management goals with PowerPoint 2010's powerful design and formatting tools.

Getting Around PowerPoint 2010

Items Seen in the PowerPoint Window

Microsoft PowerPoint works similarly to most other Microsoft Office 2010 applications in terms of window structure and basic functions. PowerPoint offers four different editing views. Change your view in the Presentation and Master Views group on the View tab.

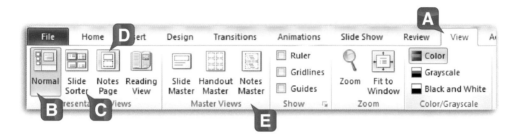

Normal View	
A View Tab	Click this tab to access the editing presentation and Master Views in PowerPoint 2010.
B Normal View	Allows access to the presentation outline, the slides, and the notes at once.
C Slide Sorter View	Shows the full presentation (all of the thumbnail slides) in this presentation focused view.
D Notes Page View	Shows a highlighted slide with its correponding notes.
E Master Views	A set of buttons that allow global/default changes to slides.

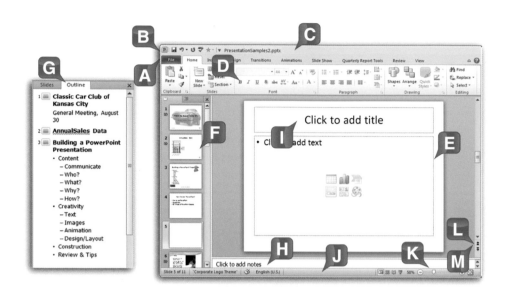

Presentation/Editing Views

A File Tab	Click this button to access the Backstage View and locate the New, Open, Save, Print, and other PowerPoint options.
B Quick Access Toolbar	Place items here for quick and easy access. The Save button is a default tool in the Quick Access toolbar. Click this button when you need to save your PowerPoint project.
C Title Bar	View the title and file type of the presentation.
D Ribbon/Tabs/Groups	Locate PowerPoint menu items and controls.
E Slide Pane	This is where your presentation text, objects, and graphics are displayed.
F Slides Thumbnail Tab	View thumbnails of all the slides in your presentation. Click on any slide in the thumbnail view to make it appear in the Slide Pane. Drag slides to rearrange their order.
G Outline Tab	View your presentation in outline format with slide titles and slide text.
H Notes Pane	Type your notes for this slide of the presentation here. You will be able to see the notes in Presenter View when you are running the slide show.
I Placeholders	Dotted borders surround placeholders for text, pictures, charts, and other objects. Click on a placeholder to add or edit content.
J Status Bar	The Status Bar is located at the bottom of the PowerPoint window and contains information such as slide number, current theme, view buttons, and a Zoom Slider.
K Zoom Slider	Zoom is the display size of a slide within the slide window. A higher zoom percentage (300%) makes everything appear larger, while a lower zoom percentage (50%) makes everything smaller. Use the plus and minus buttons to increase and decrease zoom.
L Previous Slide/	Click the Previous button to view the last slide in the presentation.
M Next Slide buttons	Click the Next button to view the next slide in the presentation.

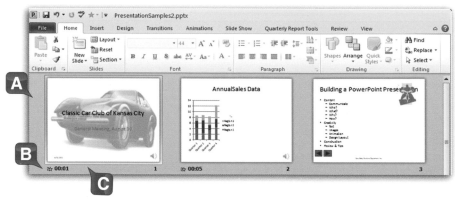

Slide Sorter View

A Thumbnail Pane	Drag thumbnails to sort and rearrange your presentation.	
B Slide Timings	Indicates the amount of time your slide show will remain on this slide before it advances.	
C Animation Icon	Indicates that there is an animation to perform on that page.	

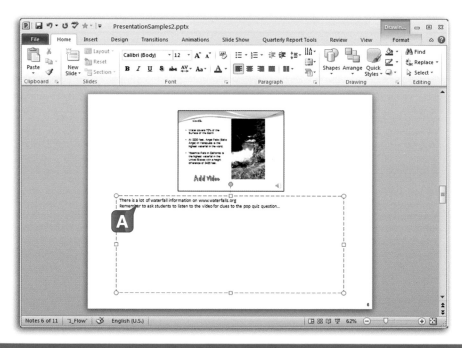

Notes Page View

A Notes Text Box	Type and edit your notes in full page view with the Notes View.

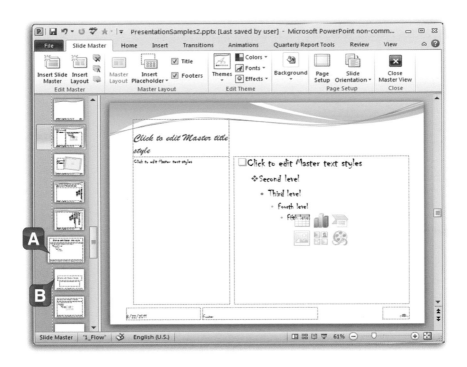

Master Views

A Slide Master	The Slide Master for a presentation determines all basic default formatting for the slides in a presentation. The Slide Master appears as a larger thumbnail in the thumbnail pane. Editing it will affect all of the layout slides below. To apply more than one theme or set of default formats, you will need to add more than one Slide Master to your presentation.
B Slide Layout	Slide Layouts are templates for new slides with a set of placeholders (such as footer, date, text boxes, and media boxes) already defined and organized on the slide for easy entry.

PowerPoint 2010 allows the user to create and edit Slide, Handout, and Notes Masters. When style changes are made to a master, every slide, notes, or handout page in your presentation is also changed.

Items You'll See on the Ribbon

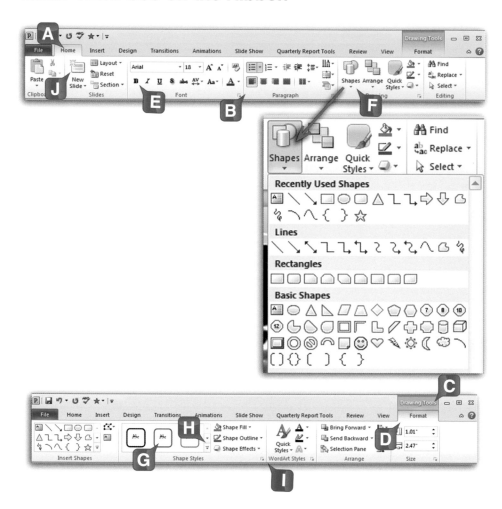

Items You'll See on the Ribbon

A Tab	Collections of related features and functions.
B Group	Collections of related controls.
C Highlighted Ribbon Section	Contextual ribbon sections appear when some objects are selected or used.
D Contextual Tabs	Some specialized tabs only appear when a particular feature is active. These special tabs usually appear in conjunction with a highlighted ribbon section.
E Slide Pane	Buttons are single-click controls that perform one function.
F Button	Some buttons have a graphic and a down-pointing arrow, while others have a default selection visible, followed by a down arrow. Clicking the arrow reveals additional choices.
G Selection Box	A panel containing a list of selectable items.
H Panel Launcher or More button	A scroll control that can be clicked to launch a selection panel.
I Dialog Box Launcher	A special group control that launches a related dialog box.
J Combo Button	These controls are split into two parts to function as both a button and a dropdown. They may be split horizontally or vertically.

Note: The Ribbon changes depending on your screen size, window size, and resolution. A small window might display only icons on the Ribbon **K**, whereas a large window might display the full text for each button or open a selection box **L**. The images shown in this book might look different from what you see on your own screen. However, icons will always remain consistent and the group names and placements will be the same (unless you have customized your Ribbon).

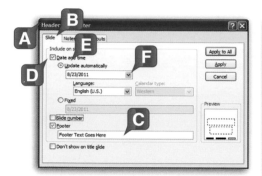

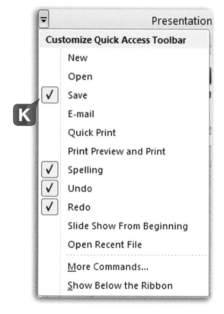

Items You'll See in Menus and Dialog Boxes

A Dialog Box	A feature-specific box that you can launch to control various functions in PowerPoint.
B Tabs	Some dialog boxes have tabs similar to the one on the ribbon. Each tab is focused on a particular subset of features.
C Text Box	A box where text can be typed.
D Check Box	A box that activates the related selection when checked and deactivates it when unchecked. More than one checkbox may be checked in a series.
E Radio Button	A circle that activates the related selection when selected and deactivates it when deselected. Only one radio button may be selected in a series.
F Dropdown Menu	A simple down-pointing arrow button that reveals a set of selectable choices.
G Right-Click Menu	This two-part menu appears when you right-click anywhere on the sheet.
H Dialog Box Launcher	In menus, buttons that launch dialog boxes are followed by ellipses (...).
I Menu Launcher	Menu selections that open additional menus are followed by right-pointing arrows.
J Shortcut Keys	Menu selections that can be launched by a keystroke on your keyboard are identified by the underlined letters in them. Click any underlined letter in a menu to launch that selection's function.
K Toggle Checkmarks	Some menus have checkmarks. Clicking an unchecked item in those lists checks it and activates the selected option. Clicking a checked item unchecks it and deactivates the selected option.

1 Insert Text Box

Difficulty: ●○○○

PROBLEM As an owner for a boutique retail shop, you have been asked to create a presentation for a small business owner's gathering. You want to show images of your store's display cases with text annotations to illustrate how you shelve and display your products. You want your text to stand out from the images and draw attention to the techniques you are discussing.

SOLUTION A text box is a shape designed to place text in a slide outside of the slide's default layout settings. Text boxes are especially useful when adding text to a graphic image.

Depending upon the application of a text box, you can either select one of the available presets, or design a custom text box by drawing and formatting the elements. Text can be added to virtually any shape inserted via the Shapes button in the Illustrations group on the Insert tab, whether they are specialized for that purpose (such as thought bubbles and call-outs) or basic figures like squares, cylinders, and stars.

See Also: Stack and Group Images

Step-by-Step

Insert Text Box

1. On the **Insert** tab in the **Text** group, click **Text Box** A. ⚡

2. Your cursor will change to a plus sign B. Click in the slide and drag to draw the text box to the size and shape you want C.

3. Type or paste the text you want to appear in the text box D.

4. The text box may be moved anywhere in the presentation by clicking and dragging (or copying/cutting and pasting) it to the preferred location. If you wish to change the size or shape of the text box, click on it, then drag any of the sizing handles E to the desired size. 💧

5. To rotate a text box, click the green rotation handle **F** and drag it in the direction you want the shape to be rotated.

 Step-by-Step

Format the Text Box

Place your cursor in the text box. The **Drawing Tools** contextual tab **H** appears on the main ribbon. By selecting the elements in the **Format** tab **I**, you can reformat the following elements of your text box:

- **Text Box Style**: Choose from styles in the **Visual Styles** selection box **J** or create your own style by making selections from the **Shape Fill** dropdown menu **K** and **Shape Outline** menu **L**.

- **Shadow and 3-D Effects:** Click the **Shape Effects** button **M** for shadow and 3-D choices.

- **Text Box Arrangement**: Adjust alignment, groupings, and rotations from the **Arrange** group **N**.

- **Size:** Manually adjust the object's size from the **Size** group **O**.

 Hot Tip: When resizing a text box (or image or WordArt objects), press and hold the **CTRL** button when dragging a sizing handle to keep the center of the object in the same place. Press and hold **SHIFT** to keep the object's proportions. Press and hold both to keep both the center and the proportions intact.

 Quickest Click: Click the **Text Box button** **G** in the **Shapes Selection Box** (or **Shapes** dropdown button) in the **Drawing** group on the **Home** tab to quickly add a text box to your slide.

 Hot Tip: You can group text boxes and images together.

2 | Format Text

Difficulty: ●○○○

PROBLEM You have been asked to prepare a presentation for next week's sales meeting. You want your text to stand out from the sales charts and draw attention to the results you are discussing.

SOLUTION By changing the default formatting of the text you have entered, you can draw attention to photo captions and information displayed on your slides. You can change the font, text size, and color, and bold or underline the text to improve the visibility and visual impact of the text being displayed.

 Step-by-Step

Change Font Typeface and Size

1. Click on the text box that contains the text you want to change.

2. Place your cursor at the place where you want your new font setting to begin, or select all of the text whose font you want to change.

3. In the **Font** group **A** on the **Home** tab, the current font and font size will be displayed. Click the dropdown arrow to open the font typeface **B** or font size **C** menus and select your desired font and font size. ⚡

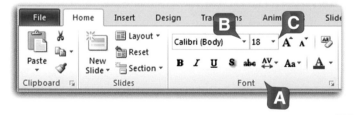

Theme Fonts **D**, those fonts associated with the theme your document is using, will be displayed at the top of the font menu. When you hover over a new font typeface or size, your document will change to let you preview the font.

4. Click the font typeface or size you want to apply the changes.

 **Step-by-Step**

Add Font Styles and Effects

1. Click on the text box that contains the text you want to change.

2. Place your cursor at the place where you want your new style to begin, or select all of the text whose style you want to change.

3. Click the **Style** or **Effect** you want to apply to your text from the **Font** group:

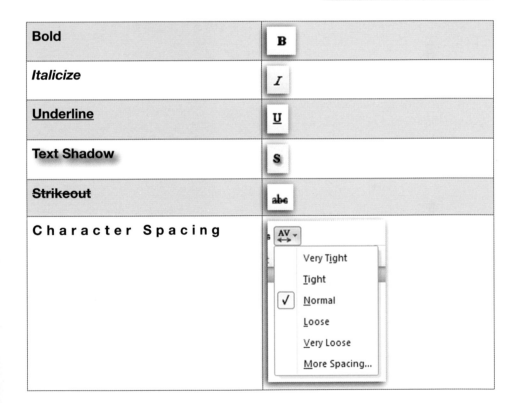

Bold	**B**
Italicize	*I*
<u>Underline</u>	<u>U</u>
Text Shadow	S
~~Strikeout~~	a̶b̶c̶
C h a r a c t e r S p a c i n g	AV ▾

For Character Spacing the dropdown menu shows:

- Very Tight
- Tight
- ✓ Normal
- Loose
- Very Loose
- More Spacing...

 CONTINUE

cHANGE cASE	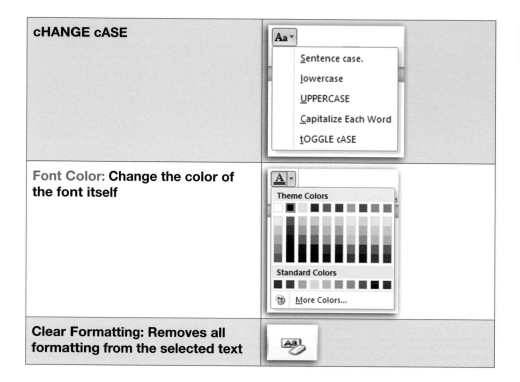
Font Color: Change the color of the font itself	
Clear Formatting: Removes all formatting from the selected text	

Quickest Click: To increase or decrease a font size a point increment at a time, select the text you want to change, then click the **Increase Font Size E** or **Decrease Font Size F** button.

Quickest Click: Copy Formatting. Select the text with the formatting you want to copy, then click the **Format Painter** button  in the **Clipboard** group on the **Home** tab. Apply the copied formatting by selecting the text you want formatted. Double-click the **Format Painter** button to apply the copied formatting to multiple selections of text. Click on **Format Painter** again to end copy formatting.

Hot Tip: Find additional text formatting options by clicking the dialog box launcher **H** in the Font group. Check the box by the formatting option you want, then click **OK**.

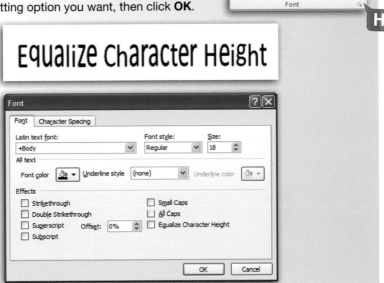

3 | Use an Existing Theme

Difficulty: ●○○○

PROBLEM As one of many coworkers who share information created in multiple Microsoft programs, you want documents that you create to have the same look and feel from one program to the next and one person to the next.

SOLUTION Use an Existing Theme. In the past, it took time to format documents to match each other because you had to choose color or style options for your tables, charts, shapes, and diagrams separately. Themes simplify the process of creating coordinated, professional-looking documents. The same themes are available in all Microsoft Office programs. You can easily apply a theme to give all of your office's items a consistent, branded look.

Step-by-Step

View and Apply a Theme

1. Open the presentation you want to edit.

2. On the **Design** tab, in the **Themes** group you will see a selection box of **Theme** examples **A**. Click the down arrow on the scroll bar located to the right of these examples **B** to see the next row of available themes, or click the **More** button **C** to open the **All Themes** menu. Your current theme choice will be listed at the top under **This Presentation** **D**.

Even more themes are available from Microsoft Office Online under the **From Office.com** heading on the **Themes** gallery . You will need an internet connection to view and download these themes.

3. Hover your cursor over a theme. Your document will change so you can preview that theme.

4. Click the theme you want to apply. The new theme will be applied to ALL slides in the presentation.

Bright Idea: Create consistent, polished, and professional looking presentations by using the same theme for your Excel, PowerPoint, and Word documents.

Caution: If you are changing a theme after you have already entered text and images, you need to check through every slide to make sure the changes did not create layout problems .

4 | Create a Custom Theme

Difficulty: ●●○○

PROBLEM As the regional sales manager for an auto parts manufacturer, you make several presentations a month using PowerPoint. You want to change the theme so that it matches your company's colors, so that the fonts used match up with the fonts used in your MS Word documents.

SOLUTION Creating a custom theme will enable you to take a standard Office theme and modify it to your liking. Find a standard theme that has a look that you like, and then modify it by changing the colors, the fonts, or the line and fill effects. You can then save it as your very own custom theme.

Step-by-Step

Create a Theme Color Set

There are 12 Theme Color placeholders that determine the colors for body text, background color, accent text, and hyperlink text. Each placeholder needs to be assigned a certain color.

1. On the **Design** tab, in the **Themes** group, click the theme **Colors** dropdown button .

2. Choose **Create New Theme Colors** B at the bottom of the **Colors** dropdown menu to open the **Create New Theme Colors** dialog box.

3. Each placeholder is listed with the current color selected beside it. Click on the color box and choose your desired color **C**. You can see how the styles and colors that you choose will look under the **Sample** pane **D**.

4. Repeat this step for all placeholders.

5. In the **Name:** box **E**, type a name for the color scheme.

6. Click **Save** to apply the new color set. These color settings will now be available from the **Colors** dropdown button in the **Theme** group **F**.

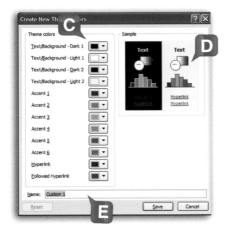

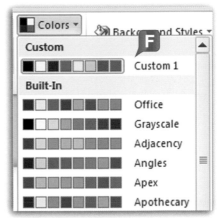

Step-by-Step

Create Theme Font Set

1. On the **Design** tab, in the **Theme** group, click the theme **Fonts** button **G**.

2. Select **Create New Theme Fonts** **H** at the bottom of the dropdown menu to launch the **Create New Theme Fonts** dialog box.

3. Use the dropdown menus to select **Heading** and **Body** fonts **I**. You can see how the fonts you choose will look under the **Sample** pane **J**.

4. In the **Name** box **K**, type a name for the new font set.

5. Click **Save** to create new font set. These font settings will now be available from the **Fonts** dropdown button in the **Themes** group **L**.

Create a Custom Theme 11

Step-by-Step

Save a Custom Theme

1. When you have your color, font, and style settings customized the way you want them, click the **More** button **M** in the **Themes** group on the **Design** tab to open the **All Themes** dialog box.

2. Select **Save Current Theme** **N** to open the **Save Current Theme** dialog box.

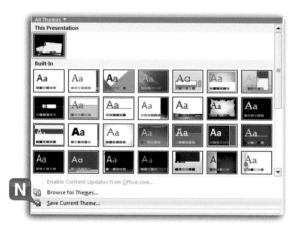

3. Type a name for your theme in the **File name:** text box **O**.

4. Click **Save**.

Step-by-Step

Choose and Apply a Custom Theme

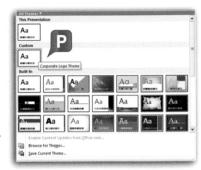

1. On the **Design** tab, in the **Themes** group, click the **More** button **M** in the scroll bar to open the **All Themes** menu.

2. Your custom theme will be available under the **Custom** heading **Q**.

3. Click on the custom theme to apply it to your presentation. 彙

 Hot Tip: To open a custom theme directly from your hard drive or network drive, click **Browse for Themes** **Q** in the **All Themes** menu to open the **Choose theme or Themed Document** dialog box.

Browse to locate the folder where your theme file is located, click the file you want, then click **Apply**.

 Quickest Click: Recently used Themes, including your custom themes, will appear in the selection box on the **Design** tab in the **Themes** group.

5 | Change the Background

Difficulty: ●○○○

PROBLEM You are preparing a presentation to be shown at a sales meeting and want to change the default background of your presentation to give a more striking visual effect.

SOLUTION Change the Background. Changing the background allows you to customize the look and feel of your presentation by choosing what colors are displayed or by adding a picture or other effect. You can apply the same background to a single slide, a group of slides, or the entire project.

Step-by-Step

Change Background Styles

1. On the **Design** tab in the **Background** group, click on **Background Style** **A**. This will give you 12 style options within the theme you are using. Each theme will have a different style set to choose from.

2. Click on the background of your choice to apply the background to *all* slides.

3. To change the background for only specific slides, highlight only the slides you wish **B** to change by clicking on the slide in the navigation window. Use **SHIFT +** click to select all slides in between two slides or hold **CTRL** and click on individual slides.

4. Click on **Background Styles** in the **Background** group on the **Design** tab. Right click on the background you wish to use, then select **Apply to Selected Slides** 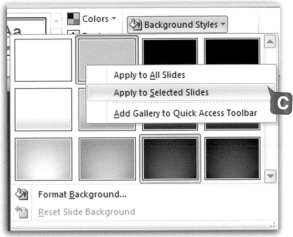.

 Hot Tip: For more background options, select **Format Background** **D** to launch the **Format Background** dialog box **E** from the **Background Styles** dropdown button.

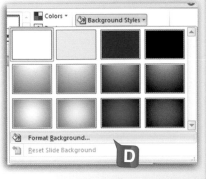

6 | Change Your Slide Layouts

Difficulty: ●●○○

PROBLEM You have recently taken a trip overseas and want to create a presentation detailing your trip with photos and captions. The default layout will do, but you want to share your photos in a nicer, cleaner manner.

SOLUTION Change your Slide Layout. Changing how the images and words appear on a slide will enable you to customize your presentation and display items in a way that matches the information you are trying to convey. By default, PowerPoint gives you the "Title Slide" layout, and information added after the first slide will be placed in the "Title and Content" layout. Clicking on the "layout" button will display the following pre-set options.

- » Title Slide
- » Title and Content
- » Section Header
- » Two Content
- » Comparison
- » Title Only
- » Blank
- » Content with Caption
- » Picture with Caption

Step-by-Step

Choose the Layout for a New Slide

1. Click on the slide in your presentation that falls just before the place where you need a new slide.

2. In the **Slides** group on the **Home** tab, click the dropdown arrow on the **New Slide** button **A**.

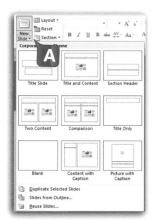

3. Click on a built-in layout option to create a new slide with that layout. It will be inserted into your presentation just after the slide you have selected.

Step-by-Step

Change the Layout on an Existing Slide

1. Select the slide or slides that you wish to change.

2. In the **Slides** group on the **Home** tab, click the **Layout** dropdown button **B**.

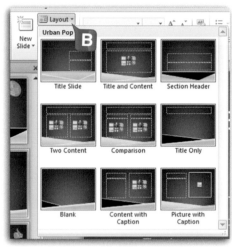

3. Click on the new layout option you want to apply to the existing content. ⚠

 Caution: If you are changing a slide's layout after you have already entered text and images, you need to make sure the changes did not create problems **C**.

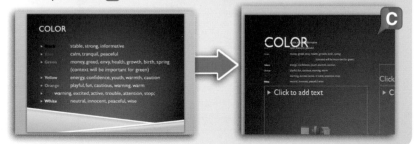

7 | Create and Save Custom Layouts

Difficulty: ●●○○

PROBLEM None of the default layout options in PowerPoint fit the presentation that you are creating. You want to create a better layout for slides that you can use both in this presentation and in others that will be similar in the future.

SOLUTION Create a Custom Layout. By creating a layout of your own, you can precisely choose the items that are shown on a slide and how they are displayed. When you are done with your layout, you can save your choices for use in the same project or at a later date.

 Step-by-Step

Create a Slide Layout

1. Click **Slide Master** A in the **Master Views** group on the **View** tab to open the **Slide Master** tab.

2. Select a layout that is similar to what you need, or select the **Blank Layout.**

3. Modify the layout:

   a. To add a placeholder to your layout, click **Insert Placeholder** B in the **Master Layout** group on the **Slide Master** tab.

   b. Click on the type of content you want your placeholder to prompt you for.

   c. Click on the slide, then drag to draw the size and location of the placeholder. To resize a placeholder, click on the placeholder, then drag by the sizing handles or corner handles C. Rotate the placeholder by clicking and dragging the green rotation handle D.

   d. To delete a placeholder, click on it, then hit the **DELETE** key.

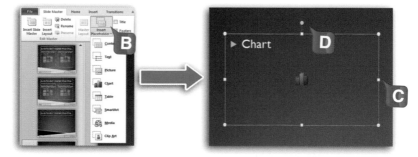

4. To rename the layout in the thumbnail list, right-click your customized layout, then select **Rename Layout** to open the **Rename Layout** dialog box.

5. Type in a name that describes your layout in the **Layout name:** textbox , then click **Rename**.

6. When you have made all the custom layouts and changes you need click the **Close Master View** button . Your custom layouts will now appear under the built-in layout options in the **New Slide** and **Layout** dropdown menus .

8 | Create a Slide Transition

Difficulty: ●●○○

PROBLEM You have finished creating the slides for tomorrow's class presentation and want to add a visually appealing way to move from one slide to the next while you are giving your lecture.

SOLUTION Slide transitions are the animation-like effects that occur in Slide Show view when you move from one slide to the next during an on-screen presentation. You can control the speed of each slide transition effect, and you can also add sound.

Step-by-Step

Insert Transitions Between Slides

1. Select the slide that you want to transition into from the thumbnail list.

2. Choose the transition effect you want from the **Transition to This Slide** group **A** on the **Transitions** tab. You will see a selection box of transition examples on the ribbon. Click the down arrow **B** to scroll through more transitions or click the **More** button **C** to view all available transitions.

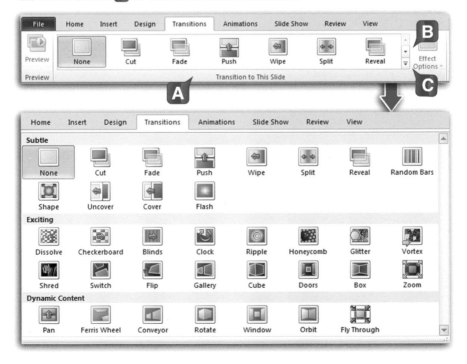

3. Click the transition you want. Your presentation will demonstrate the animation for you to preview the effect, and an animation star will appear on the slide in the thumbnail list **D**. To add the same transition for every slide in your presentation, click the **Apply to All** button **E** in the **Timing** group on the **Transitions** tab. 🔥

Step-by-Step

Change the Timing of a Transition

1. From the thumbnail list, select the slide for which you want to adjust transition timing.

2. In the **Timing** group on the **Transitions** tab, click the up or down arrows in the **Duration** box **F** to increase or decrease the amount of time a transition takes.

3. To set your presentation to advance to the next slide when you click the mouse, check the **On Mouse Click** checkbox in the **Advance Slide** menu **G**.

4. To have your presentation move to the next slide automatically, click the **After:** checkbox **H** and use the up or down arrows to set the number of seconds **I** you want to remain on the current slide. To apply the same settings for every slide in your presentation, click the **Apply to All** button. 💡

CONTINUE ▶

 Step-by-Step

Remove Slide Transitions

1. Select the slide from which you want to delete a transition in the thumbnail list.

2. Click **None** 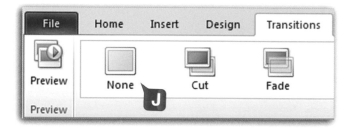 in the **Transition to This Slide** group on the **Transitions** tab. To remove transitions from every slide in your presentation, click the **Apply to All** button.

Hot Tip: You can preview your transition settings anytime by clicking the **Preview** button  on the **Transitions** tab or by clicking on the animation star beside the slide in the **Thumbnail** list.

 Bright Idea: Include transition sounds in your presentation when you are using timed slide advance. This will give you an aural cue as you are speaking that the next slide is on the screen so you don't have to keep looking at your monitor. To add a transition sound, click on the **Sound** dropdown arrow 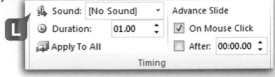 in the **Timing** group on the **Transitions** tab and select the sound you want.

9 | Add a Bookmark to an Audio or Video Clip

Difficulty: ●●○○

PROBLEM You have a presentation with an audio clip of your CEO giving a corporate vision statement to the prospective investors you are pitching. The clip is too long to use in its entirety, so you would like to play only the sections that are most relevant to your audience. You would like an easy way to jump quickly to those points in your clip, rather than clicking around or fast forwarding during your presentation.

SOLUTION Set a bookmark. PowerPoint 2010 lets you mark points of interest in a video or audio clip, making it easy to find and jump to them when giving your presentation. Bookmarks can also be used as triggers to cue animations or open other media.

See Also: Add a Video to a Presentation; Insert Audio into a Slide

Step-by-Step

1. Go to the slide that contains the audio or video clip. Click in the play control bar **A** at the place where you want your bookmark to go.

   You can also click the **Play** button **B** to listen or watch for the place where your bookmark should go. Click the **Pause** button **C** to stop the playback.

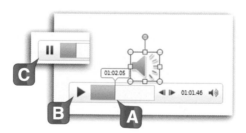

2. Click on the **Playback** tab **D** under the **Audio Tools** contextual tab, then click the **Add Bookmark** button **E** in the **Bookmarks** group. If you are adding a bookmark to a video, you will click the **Playback** tab under the **Video Tools** contextual tab.

A bookmark circle will appear in the play controls panel .

3. To view and use bookmarks, hover over the bookmark circle to see its name. Click on the bookmark circle to be able to begin playing from that point.

4. To remove a bookmark, click on it, then click the **Remove Bookmark** button **G** in the **Bookmarks** group on the **Playback** tab.

10 | Set Up Show

Difficulty: ●●●○

PROBLEM You have created your slides, carefully recorded slide advance timings, and practiced your speaking parts. You are ready to give your presentation at a conference to several workshop groups over the course of the day. When you start your slide show, you would like your slides to advance automatically in full screen mode and presenter view. Since you will be giving the same lecture several times, you would like a way to save these show settings so that you don't have to enter them every time you begin.

SOLUTION Use the Set Up Slide Show options and then save your show to a show file. PowerPoint gives you several options for how your show will run when you are ready to give your presentation. You can choose to display the show in a window on your desktop or in full screen view, for example. You can turn narrations on and off and decide whether slides will advance automatically or if you will forward them manually. When your show options are set the way you want them, you can save the presentation as a show file so that your settings will be preserved each time you play the show, or when you move the show to different computers.

Step-by-Step

1. In the **Set Up** group on the **Slide Show** tab, click the **Set Up Slide Show** button **A** to launch the **Set Up Show** dialog box.

2. Make the selections in the dialog box for the type of show you will be running:

    *   **Show type B:** Click the radio button that best matches how your show will be run.
    *   **Presented by a speaker:** Runs the show in full screen mode.
    *   **Browsed by an individual:** Runs the show in a window rather than full screen.
    *   **Browsed at a kiosk:** This setting will create a self-running presentation that restarts after it has reached the end or when the show has been idle for longer than five minutes. ⚠
    *   **Show options C:** Check the boxes that apply to your presentation.

- **Loop continuously until 'Esc':** Your presentation will return to the beginning when it reaches the end, or has been idle for longer than five minutes. This will be checked by default if **Browsed at a kiosk** is selected.

- **Show without narration:** Your show will run without playing the narration.

- **Show without animation:** Animations will be disabled in the Slide Show view.

- **Pen color:** and **Laser pointer color:** Choose the colors for these features in manual presentation modes. 🔥

- **Show slides** D: Click the **All** radio button for all slides to be included in the slide show, or click the **From** radio button to choose a range of slides.

- **Advance slides** E: Choose **Manually** to advance slides yourself during the slide show. Selecting **Using timings, if present** will advance slides based on settings you have made in the **Timing** group.

- **Multiple monitors** F: Choose which monitors your presentation will display on (if multiple are detected) and turn on **Presenter View**.

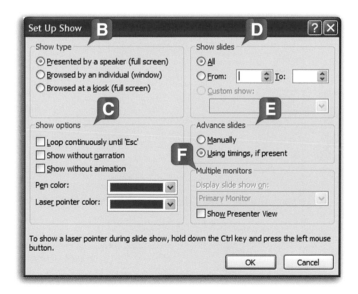

Step-by-Step

Save Your Show File

Once you are happy with your animations, timings, and triggers, you need to save the presentation as a Show File. This will embed all sound and music files into the presentation so they will be included when you move the show between computers or e-mail it to someone else.

1. Click on the **File** tab, then click **Save As** **G** to open the **Save As** dialog box.

2. Type a name for your show in the **File Name:** text box **H**.

3. Choose **PowerPointShow (*.ppsx)** **I** from the **Save as type:** dropdown menu.

4. Click **Save**.

Caution: If your presentation is going to run at a kiosk, remember that you must either set the timing options to advance the slides, or prepare action buttons for a user to click to advance the slides. Otherwise, the presentation will have no way to continue!

11 | Create Navigation Buttons to Advance Your Presentation

Difficulty: ●○○○

PROBLEM You are developing a presentation to run at a trade show. The presentation will run in a kiosk and will loop continuously. You want to offer visitors the ability to advance the show at their own speed when they interact with the kiosk.

SOLUTION Add action buttons that will advance the presentation to the next slide or return it to the previous slide.

Action buttons are shapes that you can assign an action to such as: go to another slide (next, last, first, most recent, specific slide number); go to another presentation; go to a Web page; run a program; run a macro; or play an audio clip. You can also assign actions to clip art, pictures, or SmartArt graphics.

See Also: Set Up a Show

 Step-by-Step

Add an Action Button

1. In the **Illustrations** group on the **Insert** tab, click the **Shapes** button **A** to open the dropdown menu.

2. At the bottom of the menu, under the **Actions** heading, click the **Next** action button **B**.

3. Click the place on your slide where the button will go, then drag to draw it to the size you need **C**. To change a button's size, drag by the sizing handles or corner handles. Rotate the button by clicking and dragging the green rotation handle.

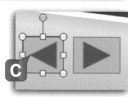

4. When you are finished drawing the button, the **Action Settings** dialog box will open. On the **Mouse Click** tab **D**, select the **Hyperlink to:** radio button **E**.

5. Select **Next Slide** from the dropdown menu **F**.

6. Click **OK**.

7. To create a back button, repeat the steps above only choose the **Back or Previous** button  in the **Shapes** menu and **Previous Slide** in the **Hyperlink to:** dropdown.

 Hot Tip: If you need navigation on *every* slide in your presentation (for a kiosk presentation, for example), you can add action buttons in **Master View.** The buttons will be added to your template and appear on every slide. *See Also: Create and Save Custom Layouts*

12 | Use Sections in PowerPoint

Difficulty: ●○○○

PROBLEM Your boss has given you the task of creating a PowerPoint presentation to show at an upcoming investor's meeting. Since the presentation covers an entire fiscal year's worth of data, you would like a way to present each quarter's financial information in its own section. You want to organize the slides so that the presentation flows well and the slides are easy to navigate.

SOLUTION Use the Sections feature to organize your slides into quarterly financial information. PowerPoint 2010 introduced a new feature that allows you to name sections and organize slides into groups, much like you organize documents into file folders.

Step-by-Step

Add and Name a Section

1. In the **Normal** or **Slide Sorter** view, right-click in the thumbnail list between the two slides where your section will begin.

2. Click on **Add Section** from the fly-out menu **A**. A section divider will appear in the thumbnail list with the name **Untitled Section B**, and all the slides associated with that section will be highlighted.

3. Right-click on the **Untitled Section** divider and then choose **Rename Section C** from the fly-out menu to open the **Rename Section** dialog box.

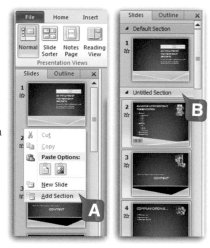

4. Type a name for your section in the **Section name:** text box **D**.

Bright Idea: Use Presentation Sections when you are working on a presentation with several people. Each team member can arrange their slides within a specific section and still keep the overall presentation organized. You can also use Sections to create sales and marketing templates to help your team create consistent and effective presentations.

Hot Tip: To move, delete, or collapse and expand a section, right-click on the section you want to change, then select the appropriate option.

13 | Adjust Screen Resolution

Difficulty: ●○○○

PROBLEM You are giving a presentation in a conference room that has an older projection system. Your new laptop runs at a higher screen resolution than the projector supports, so the image on the screen is distorted and part of it is chopped off.

SOLUTION Change the resolution for your slide show. PowerPoint 2010 offers the option to set the resolution a slide show is displayed at. This is particularly good for full screen slide shows that will look the best if the resolution settings are compatible.

Step-by-Step

Change the Screen Resolution for Your Slide Show

1. On the **Slide Show** tab in the **Monitors** group, click the arrow on the **Resolution:** box  to open the dropdown menu. The default will be set to **Use Current Resolution.**

2. Choose the resolution you need for your monitor or projector.

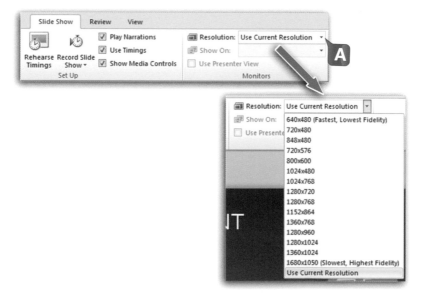

Hot Tip: Lower resolutions run faster but may not give you the best quality. Choose the best resolution for your slide show by setting the highest resolution supported that runs fast enough. Most projectors support a maximum of 1024x768.

14 Set Up Headers and Footers

Difficulty: ●○○○

PROBLEM You are creating a presentation for a company retreat. There will be many lectures over the course of the week, and all the employees will be receiving many handouts from presentations and vendors. You want a way to make sure that your slides and handouts will quickly identify you and your presentation.

SOLUTION Add a header and footer to your slides and handouts that displays the title of your lecture and all the information you want the students to remember (such as contact information) when they refer to their notes at a later date.

Headers and footers refer to the text or data (such as slide number, page number, date, etc.) that you want to appear at the top or bottom of your slides. Instead of adding this type of information on every slide or page manually, you can add it once and set it to apply to all your slides or pages.

Step-by-Step

Add a Footer to a Slide

1. Select the slide that needs a header or footer, then click the **Header & Footer** button **A** in the **Text** group on the **Insert** tab to open the **Header and Footer** dialog box.

2. On the **Slide** tab **B**, click the **Footer** checkbox **C**, and then enter the text that you want to appear in the footer in the text box **D**. (Note: If you do *not* want the footer to appear on the title slide, make sure the **Don't show on title slide** checkbox **E** is selected.)

3. You can also add **Slide number** **F** and the date **G** to your slides from this dialog box by clicking the corresponding checkboxes.

4. Click **Apply**. To have the footer text appear on all slides in the presentation, click **Apply to All**.

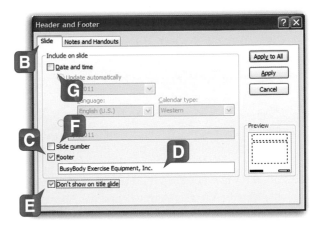

![Step-by-Step icon] **Step-by-Step**

Add a Header or Footer to Notes and Handouts

Optional: There are two good ways to add headers and footers to your **Notes** and **Handouts**:

From the Header and Footer dialog box

This option offers you a quick way to add a consistent header and footer across all your presentation documents.

1. On the **Insert** tab in the **Text** group, click the **Header & Footer** button  to launch the **Header and Footer** dialog box.

2. Click the **Notes and Handouts** tab 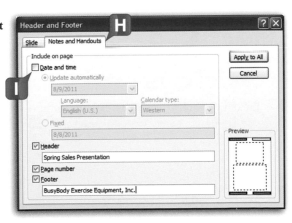.

3. Select the checkbox beside **Header** or **Footer** and then type the text you want to appear on your notes pages or handouts in the textbox. From this dialog box, you can also add and define a date to your **Notes** and **Handouts** by clicking the **Date and time** checkbox [I].

4. Click **Apply to All**.

The text you have added will appear in the header and footer positions on both handouts and notes.

In the Handout or Notes Master View

This option lets you edit headers and footers directly on the **Handout** or **Notes Master**. In **Master View** you can change the location and size of header and footer placeholders and specify different text for **Notes** and **Handouts**.

1. On the **View** tab, click the **Handout Master** [J] or **Notes Master** button [K] in the **Master Views** group to open the **Notes Master** or **Handout Master** tab.

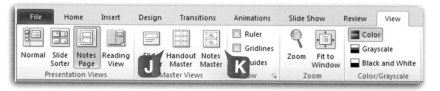

2. Make sure the **Header** or **Footer** checkbox [L] is selected in the **Placeholders** group. Click inside the Header or Footer placeholder box on the master [M] and type the text you want.

To change the size or location of the placeholder, click on the placeholder box, then drag by the sizing handles or corner handles [N]. Rotate the box by clicking and dragging the green rotation handle.

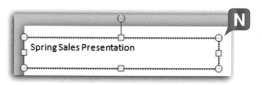

3. From this view, you can also add page numbers [O] and the date [P] to your Notes and Handouts by clicking the corresponding checkboxes.

4. When your changes are complete, click **Close Master View** [Q] to return to your presentation.

Quickest Click: When you want to add dates or slide numbers, click the **Slide Number** or **Date & Time** buttons in the **Text** group on the **Insert** tab to quickly open the **Header and Footer** dialog box.

15 | Create an Interactive Activity

Difficulty: ●●●○

PROBLEM You want to set up an interactive presentation, in the form of a game show, to help your students prepare for an upcoming test.

SOLUTION Set up triggers, action buttons, and hyperlinks for students to click as they go through the game show. Animations, pictures, and text can all have a trigger associated with them. For example, clicking on an image, viewing an animation, or entering text links to an event, such as moving to another slide, displaying a correct answer, or showing another animation. Using triggers adds surprise to your slides while providing a way for your viewer to participate in your presentation, rather than just watch it.

Step-by-Step

Create a Jeopardy-style Game with Action Buttons and Hyperlinks

Start by opening a new presentation and populate it with several blank slides. Choose a simple or plain theme that won't interfere visually with your objects and action buttons.

Set up your game "board"

1. Add shapes to make the main "board" or home slide. The shapes will link to question-and-answer slides. To add a shape to your slide, open the **Shapes** dropdown menu  in the **Illustrations** group on the **Insert** tab and select the shape you need. This example uses rectangles. Type appropriate text into each shape. Repeat until your board is complete. *See Also: Add a Shape to Your Slide*

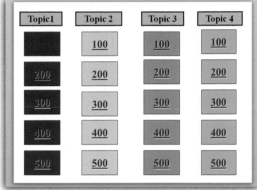

Create your question and answer slides.

2. Make sure there is a question-and-answer slide for each link on your board slide **B**. Add a shape to display the question or clue **C**, and then another shape to reveal the answer **D** once the player has had a chance to guess or give up.

3. Select the question shape **C**, then click the **Animations** tab. Add an animation that will reveal the shape only after a click (or a certain amount of time, if you wish) **E**.

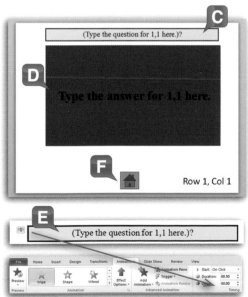

4. Add an image or shape on each question-and-answer slide that will return you to the board slide. In this example, the image is a clipart image of a house **F**.

Link your slides

5. Return to your home "board" slide and select a game shape. Select the shape that you want to become a link to the question-and-answer slide, then click on the **Insert** tab.

6. In the **Links** group, click the **Action** button **G** to open the **Action Settings** dialog box.

7. On the **Mouse Click** tab, click the **Hyperlink to:** radio button **H**, then click the down arrow to open the menu. Select **Slide…** **I** to open the **Hyperlink to Slide** dialog box, then choose the slide you want to link to from the **Slide title:** pane **J**. The preview pane will show an image of the slide you have chosen.

8. Click **OK** to close the **Hyperlink to Slide** dialog box. If you want to add additional actions such as sound to your action button, make those adjustments in the **Action Settings** dialog box, then click **OK**. Repeat for all the shapes on your game "board." *See Also: Insert a Hyperlink into a Presentation*

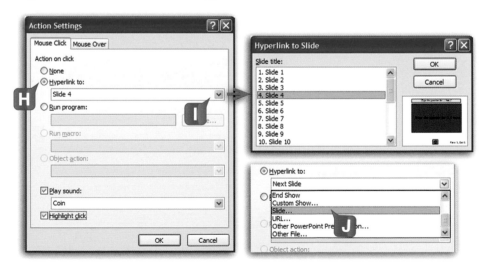

Link back to the home, board slide

9. Follow the steps above to create an action button that links back to your home board slide from every question-and-answer slide 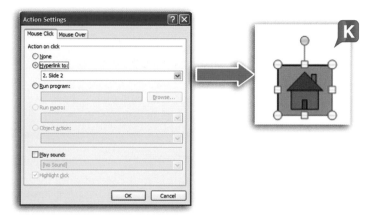.

Bright Idea: This is just one example of a game that can be created using action buttons. Search the Web for many more ideas and templates for PowerPoint Interactive Games and interactive training presentations.

16 | Animate Text and Images

Difficulty: ●●○○

PROBLEM You are giving a presentation with slides that offer several bullet points for each topic. You want a way to introduce one bullet at a time so your audience is not reading ahead, but you don't want to have to create a new slide for each point.

SOLUTION Animate the text on your slide so that each bullet point will appear based on the trigger that you choose. Using animations in your PowerPoint presentation is a great way to control the pacing of your information. You can apply effects to add objects to your slides based on a trigger or timing specifications. You can remove objects in the same fashion or add an effect that will call attention to the object you want to emphasize as you speak. Multiple effects can be added to the same object.

There are four kinds of animation effects in PowerPoint 2010:

Entrance Effects – An animation that introduces your content onto the screen. Choices include fade in, fly in from an edge, bounce in, and more. Good for introducing bullet lists and controlling the pacing to match your speaking pace.

Exit Effects – An animation that removes content from the presentation. Choices include fly off, fade out/disappear, spiral off, and more. Exit effects might be used when demonstrating the best choice from a list of options, asking multiple-choice questions (wrong answers are removed), or working through a checklist.

Emphasis Effects – An animation that calls attention to content on the screen in some way. Choices include making an object change color, shrink, grow, flash, or spin, among others. These are good for directing your audience's attention to the most important content on the slide. You can also use emphasis effects for the same reasons as entrance and exit effects.

Motion Paths – An animation that causes an object to move up or down, left or right, in a pattern, and more. Use Motion Path animations when you want to visually connect objects to other objects (two images fly together), or when you want to visually demonstrate a workflow or information flow concept (content moves from one step to the next, etc.).

Caution: Animations should be used sparingly and only when they will truly enhance your message. Too many animations on a single slide can be distracting rather than informative, and your audience will tire quickly of animations on every slide.

Step-by-Step

Add Animation to a Text Object

1. Navigate to the slide you want to enhance with animations. Highlight the specific text you want affected by the animation **A**, then click the **Animations** tab.

2. Choose the style of animation you want in the **Effects Selection Box B** in the **Animation** group. Click the up and down arrows to browse the list of animations, or click the **More** button **C** to see all available options at once. When you mouse over an animation option, your slide will perform the animation for you to preview.

3. Click on the animation style to apply it to your highlighted text. A numbered tag **D** will appear beside the text (when **Animations** tab is selected only). This indicates the order in which your animations will be played on the slide.

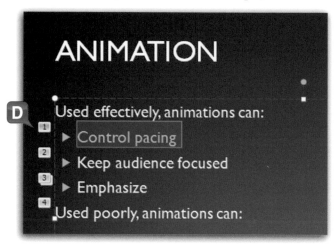

4. When you select an animation, more effect options are offered to you from the **Effect Options** dropdown button **E**. Click this button to specify details about how your effect will display **F**.

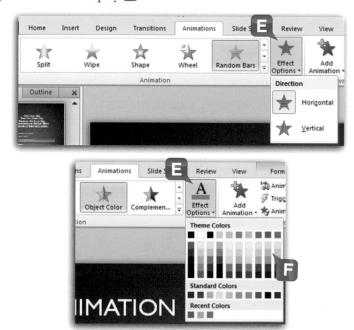

 Step-by-Step

Add Multiple Animations to the Same Object

1. Make sure the text is still highlighted, then click the **Add Animation** button G in the **Advanced Animation** group on the **Animations** tab.

2. Make your selection for additional animations from the dropdown menu. When multiple animations are applied to the same object or block of text, the **Multiple** button **H** will be highlighted for that object in the **Animations** selection box, and the numbered tags will appear as a stacked set of tags **I**.

Edit Animation Timings

1. Make sure the text is still highlighted. You can set start, duration, and delay timing for an animation in the **Timing** group on the **Animations** tab.
   - Choose when an animation will begin by selecting an option from the **Start:** dropdown menu **J**.
   - Specify how long the effect will take in the **Duration:** box **K**. A short number will move the animation quickly across the screen. A long number will slow the animation down.
   - Set a delay by entering the number of seconds you want an animation to wait before it begins in the **Delay:** box **L**.

Bright Idea: Always preview your animations before you move on!

Hot Tip: These same steps work for images, shapes, and other objects.

17 | Motion Path Animations

Difficulty: ●●○○

PROBLEM As part of your presentation highlighting the success of your college's track team this season, you want the text on certain slides to follow a path across the screen from left to right.

SOLUTION Apply a Motion Path Animation. Within PowerPoint, you can add either a predefined path for an animated object to follow across the screen, or define your own custom path.

Step-by-Step

Apply a Motion Path Animation to Text or an Object

1. Highlight the text, or click the object, that needs a Motion Path and then click the **Animations** tab.

2. In the **Animation** group, click the **More** button **A** on the selection window to open the dropdown menu. Scroll to the bottom of the menu until you see the **Motion Paths** heading **B**. 💧

3. Choose from **Lines, Arcs, Turns, Shapes, or Loops** to describe the type of motion you want your object to take. Click on your choice. Your slide will play the animation for you to preview and the path will appear on your slide as two arrows connected by a dotted line .

4. Adjust the path's beginning by clicking on the **Green** arrow and dragging where you want your animation to start. Click the **Red** arrow and drag it to where you want your animation to end. ● Test your animation by clicking the **Preview** button on the **Animations** tab D or the **Play** button on the **Animation Pane** E.

To move the whole path, click on it when the mouse pointer displays a four-way arrow F, then drag the path where you want it.

Step-by-Step

Create a Custom Motion Path

1. Highlight the text, or click the object, that needs a **Motion Path** and then click **Custom Path** G from **Animation** selection box.

 CONTINUE

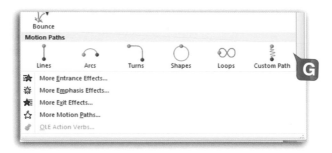

2. Click where you want the motion to start, then:

- **To draw a path of straight lines** 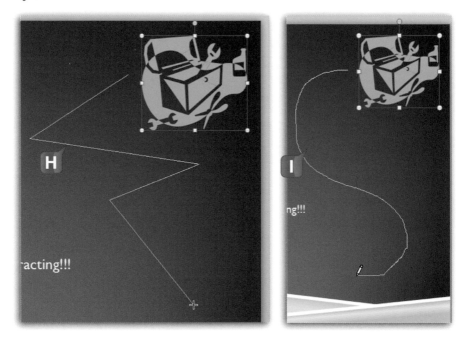 **H** – Click where you want the path to start, then click where you want the straight line to end. Continue until your path is complete, then double-click to end the path.

- **To draw an irregular path** **I** – Click where you want to start, then hold down the left mouse button while you draw a path. Double-click to end the path.

Test your animation by clicking the **Preview** button on the **Animations** tab **D** or the **Play** button on the **Animation Pane** **E**.

Hot Tip: For more pre-set motion path options, click the **More Motion Paths...** menu option  in the Animations selection box to open the **Change Motion Path** dialog box.

Hot Tip:

Tips for Motion Paths

- The **center** of an object or text bullet follows the motion path. Position your start and end arrows so that the center of your object will be placed correctly. You may need to adjust a motion path several times to get an image or text box to line up just right.

- If your path is not closed (object does not return to its starting point), position the object that will move at the motion path's starting point. For example: if your logo swooshes in from off the slide, move the image off the slide in **Normal** view. This will prevent the image from jumping around when you play your slideshow.

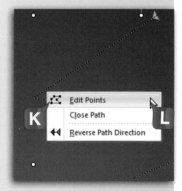

- Right-click any motion path, then select **Edit Points** K from the menu to reveal black handles that will allow you to adjust your path.

- To make an object return to its starting point after creating a custom path, right-click on the path, then select **Close Path** L. PowerPoint will add a final line to the path that returns the object to the starting point.

18 Animate a Chart

Difficulty: ●○○○

PROBLEM You are preparing a presentation for your manager that will show your sales team's quarterly profit numbers using a graphical chart. The chart is organized by Quarter and Region, but you want to discuss the data a region at a time.

SOLUTION Animate your chart to reveal each group of numbers in sequence rather than show the entire chart at the beginning.

Step-by-Step

1. Insert your chart and data using the **Insert Chart** button **A** in the **Illustrations** group on the **Insert** tab.

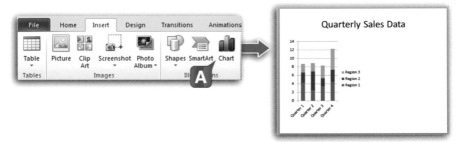

2. When your chart is ready, select the chart, then click the **Animations** tab.

3. Choose the style of animation you want from the **Animations** selection box **B** in the **Animation** group on the **Animations** tab.

4. Click on the **Effect Options** button 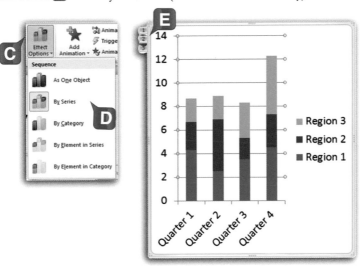 **C** to open the dropdown menu and choose **By Series** **D** to animate each region's data individually. A number tab will appear for each series **E** beside your chart (in **Animations** tab only).

5. Adjust the **Start** timing and set **Duration** and **Delay** times as needed in the **Timing** group **F** on the **Animations** tab. *See Also: Animate Text and Images*

Your chart data will appear a region at a time as specified by your timing settings and triggers.

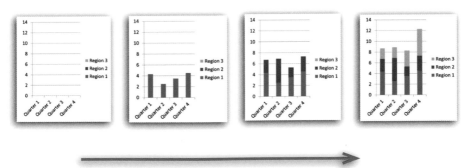

STOP

19 | Animate a SmartArt Graphic

Difficulty: ●●○○

PROBLEM You have been hired by a small health news magazine to help them reorganize their reporting structure. You want to create a presentation that walks your client through the new organization a reporting level at a time, giving you time to explain the responsibilities of each manager as you go.

SOLUTION Animate a SmartArt graphic. SmartArt graphics give you powerful visual tools to illustrate complicated structures such as organization charts, processes, and relationships. You can add even more power to these illustrations by animating sections of a SmartArt graphic to appear when you need them in your presentation.

Animations for SmartArt graphics are different from other objects in a few key ways:

- Connecting lines are not animated individually and are always associated with the shape that follows the connector.

- Shapes are animated in the order that they appear in the graphic—you can reverse the sequence of animations, but you cannot animate shapes out of order.

- Some effects are not available for SmartArt graphics. Those that are unavailable will appear grayed out in menus.

Step-by-Step

Animate SmartArt Shapes

1. Select the SmartArt graphic that you want to animate, then click on the **Animations** tab.

2. Choose the style of animation you want in the **Effects Selection Box** **A** in the **Animation** group. Click the up and down arrows to browse the list of animations, or click the **More** button **B** to see all available options at once. When you mouse over an animation option, your slide will perform the animation for you to preview.

3. Click the **Effect Options** button **C** to open the dropdown menu.

4. To animate a level at a time on an organization chart, select **Level at Once**  from the dropdown menu under the **Sequence** heading. Other effects options include:

   - **As One Object**: The whole SmartArt graphic is treated as one large object.

   - **All at Once**: All of the shapes within the SmartArt graphic are animated at the same time, but each object within the graphic performs the animation (as opposed to the graphic performing the animation as a whole). Use rotation or grow animation styles with this option.

   - **One by One**: Each shape within the graphic is animated separately.

   - **Level One by One**: The shapes within the SmartArt graphic are animated first by level and then individually within that level.

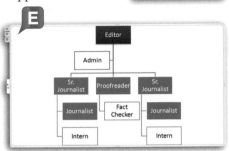

5. A number tab will appear for each level  beside your SmartArt graphic (in **Animations** tab only).

6. Adjust the **Start** time and set **Duration** and **Delay** times as needed in the **Timing** group  on the **Animations** tab. *See Also: Animate Text and Images*

   Your SmartArt graphic will display one organizational level at a time as specified by your timing settings and triggers.

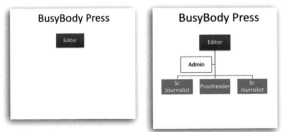

20 | View and Re-Order Animations

Difficulty: ●●○○

PROBLEM As you preview the text and image animations that you have created for your project, you discover several that would work better in a different order than they're currently displaying.

SOLUTION By using the Animation task pane, you can edit, view, and change the order of animations that you have added to your text and images.

Step-by-Step

Use the Animation Task Pane to Re-Order Animations

1. Select the slide you want to work with, then click the **Animation Pane** button **A** in the **Advanced Animation** group on the **Animations** tab to open the **Animation Pane B**.

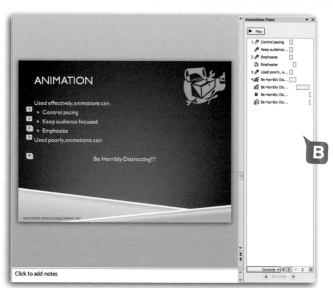

In this task pane, the order that the effects will play are indicated by numbers **C** that correspond to the numbered tags on the slide display. Icons **D** represent the type of animation effect and rectangular timeline bars **E** represent the duration of the effects.

When an effect is selected, the effect is highlighted and a dropdown arrow appears **F**.

2. Click on an animation you wish to move, then click the up or down Re-Order buttons **G** at the bottom of the **Animation Pane** to move the effect up or down the list.

3. To make further edits from the **Animation Pane**, select the animation you wish to edit, then click the down arrow to open the menu **F**. From here you can change the start time options, **H** open effect and timing dialog boxes, or remove the animation. *See Also: Animate Text and Images.*

4. Test your changes before closing pane by clicking the **Play** button **I**.

5. Click the **Close** button **J** to dismiss the **Animation Pane** when you are finished working with animations.

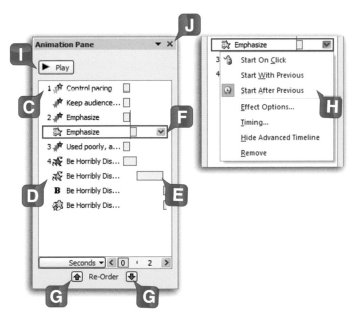

21 | Preview an Animation

Difficulty: ●○○○

PROBLEM You have completed preparing a complicated animation of text and images on one of your most important slides in your sales and marketing presentation to the president of your company. You want to preview the animations in order to make sure that they work correctly before you begin your talk.

SOLUTION There are several ways to preview animations once you have made your changes. PowerPoint will play animations for you to preview when you hover over animations options in the **Animations** selection box, but once your settings have been chosen, it is always a good idea to make sure that slides are going to perform the way you expect.

Step-by-Step

Test Your Animations

1. Select the slide you wish to preview.

2. Click the **Preview** button **A** at the far left of the **Animations** tab or click the **Play** button **B** on the **Animation** pane.

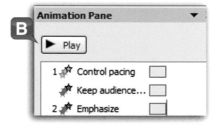

Quickest Click: Click the animation icon  located beside the slide's thumbnail in **Normal View** to have PowerPoint play the animations for that slide.

Bright Idea: If you wish to preview your animations as they will play in slide show view, click on the **Slide Show** button  in the **Status Bar** at the bottom right corner of your window. PowerPoint will switch to slide show view, beginning on the slide you currently have selected. Watch the animations or click the triggers to test your slide, then hit **ESCAPE** to return to edit view.

STOP

22 | Set a Trigger on a Video or Audio Bookmark

Difficulty: ●●●○

PROBLEM You want to reinforce a video demonstration of a science lesson with text bullets that appear at the appropriate times.

SOLUTION Set a trigger on a bookmark. Bookmark Triggers allow you to activate events such as moving to another slide, displaying a correct answer, or showing another animation based on reaching a specific (bookmarked) point in a video or audio clip.

See Also: Add a Video to a Presentation; Insert Audio into a Slide; Add a Bookmark to an Audio or Video Clip; Animate Text and Images

Step-by-Step

1. Select the object or text that will be affected by your animation. If you have not already done so, add the animation that you want the object to perform.

2. Open the **Animation Pane** by clicking the **Animation Pane** button **A** in the **Advanced Animation** group on the **Animations** tab.

3. In the **Animation Pane**, select the animation that you want the bookmark to trigger **B**.

4. In the **Advanced Animation** group, open the **Trigger** dropdown menu **C**, select **On Bookmark D**, then click the bookmark from the list that will trigger the animation **E**.

T he **Animation Pane** will change to list your triggers **F**, and the numbered tags on your slide (in **Animations** tab only) will change to trigger icons **G**. In this example, the three waterfall facts will appear as the video passes the three bookmarks on the play control panel **H**.

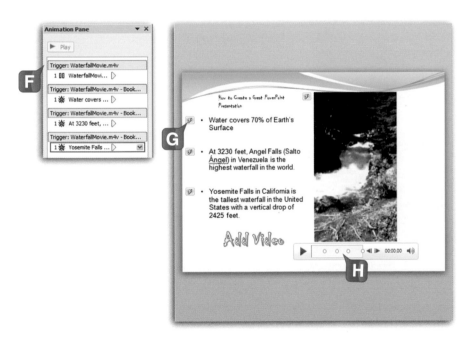

23 | Add a Video to a Presentation

Difficulty: ●●○○

PROBLEM While preparing a presentation for potential investors at a trade show booth, you want to include a short video clip greeting from your company's CEO. Furthermore, as you move through your presentation, you want to link to several other videos located on your company's website.

SOLUTION PowerPoint 2010 lets you add video clips from files located on your computer, Flash movies, or links to video sources located on the internet. Once your video is included, you can also choose whether to have the video play in a window or in full-screen, and whether or not the video will start automatically or when a viewer clicks on the screen.

> **Option:** There are several different ways you can include video in a PowerPoint presentation. You will need to choose the best way that fits the needs and resources of your venue. For example: do not link to a video on a website if you will not have internet connectivity at your lecture. Similarly, if you want to show several videos, you may want to avoid massive file sizes and slow performance by embedding each video directly into your presentation.

Step-by-Step

Embed a Video File

In PowerPoint 2010, you can embed a video file directly into your presentation. Embedding a video means the files are automatically included in the presentation so you don't have to worry about a missing file when you are in the middle of delivering the presentation. Embedding the media also makes it easier to email or copy a complete presentation to other people.

PowerPoint 2010 will support QuickTime (.mov and .mp4) and Adobe Flash (.swf) when you have installed the QuickTime and Adobe Flash players. Note: Some editing features are not available when using Flash in PowerPoint 2010.

1. Click to the slide that will display the video, then click the **Insert** tab.
2. In the **Media** group, click the dropdown arrow on the **Video** button **A**.
3. Select **Video from file B** to open the **Insert Video** dialog box. ✳
4. Browse to the file you want to embed, select it, then click the **Insert** button **C** to embed the video into the slide. A thumbnail of the first frame and video controls bar **F** will appear on your slide.

Step-by-Step

Link to a Video File

Creating a link to, rather than embedding, a video file can dramatically reduce the file size of your presentation. You will need to make sure that the video files are sent in addition to the presentation file if you are sharing or emailing the presentation. They will not be automatically combined with the presentation. 💡

1. Click to the slide that will display the video, then click the **Insert** tab.

2. In the **Media** group, click the dropdown arrow on the **Video** button **A**.

3. Select **Video from file B** to open the **Insert Video** dialog box.

4. Browse to the file you want to embed, select it, then click the down arrow to the right of the **Insert** button **D**.

5. Select **Link to File E**. A thumbnail of the first frame and video controls bar **F** will appear on your slide.

Step-by-Step

Link to a Video on a Web Site

Your presentation may require that you show a video that is hosted on a web site external to your own hard drive or intranet. Sites such as YouTube or Hulu will provide you with the embed codes for playing a video from your presentation. (Note: "Embed code" is the term used by video web sites to create an external link to their content. In this context, it is *not* the same as embedding a video *file*.)

1. Browse to the web site that contains the video you want to link to and copy the embed code **G** for the video you plan to link to. This example will use a YouTube embed code.

   Note: YouTube offers you options for how the video will be displayed. After you click the **Share** button, check the **Use old embed code** checkbox, then choose the display size for your video. These changes will be reflected in the embed code. These instructions will be different for each video website. You will need to follow the directions on the site you plan to use.

2. Click on the slide that will display the video, then click the **Insert** tab.

3. In the **Media** group, click the dropdown arrow on the **Video** button **A**.

4. Select **Video from Web Site H** to open the **Insert Video from Web Site** dialog box.

5. Paste your copied embed code into the text box **I**.

6. Click **Insert**. The video will appear as an empty, black box on your slide. When the presentation is run, the video will play inside a YouTube (or other site-specific) wrapper . ⚠

 Quickest Click: Click the **Insert Media Clip** button on a new content slide to quickly insert a video or audio clip.

 Bright Idea: To prevent confusion and broken links, make it a habit to save or copy your media files into the *same* folder as your presentation file before you link them to a slide. This will make it easier to copy all the media that is associated with your presentation when moving or emailing the presentation.

 Caution: If you link to a video on an external website (or drive, etc.), make sure you will have internet connectivity at the venue where you will be presenting.

24 Insert Audio into a Slide

Difficulty: ●●○○

PROBLEM You're having the parents of several students from your music class over for dinner, and you've planned a slide show of the students' latest recital. For this music-oriented evening, the slide show would be improved if you could add the music from the recital in the background.

SOLUTION You can enhance your presentation by adding video or audio to the slides. Music is an effective way to introduce or end a presentation and it gives your audience something to listen to as they enter and leave the presentation room. You could play a movie theme song as background music for several slides, or play a voice recording that contains advertising slogans to insert on a single slide, for example.

Step-by-Step

1. Click on the slide that will play the audio clip, then click the **Insert** tab.

2. In the **Media** group, click the dropdown arrow on the **Audio** button **A**.

3. Select **Audio from File B** to open the **Insert Audio** dialog box. 🔹

4. Browse to the file you want to insert, select it, then click the **Insert** button **C**.

The audio icon  **D** will appear on your slide. Mouse over or click on the icon to reveal the audio controls bar **E**.

Step-by-Step

Edit Playback Settings for an Audio Clip

1. Follow the directions above to insert your audio clip onto a slide.

2. Click the audio icon to open the **Audio Tools** contextual tab **F**, then click the **Playback** tab **G**.

   From this tab, you can change how the clip will play and interact with your presentation. Some common useful settings are:

   - **Volume**: Click the **Volume** dropdown button **H** to open a menu for how loudly or softly your audio will play.

   - **Start**: Click the dropdown button on the **Start** menu **I** to set a start time for the audio.

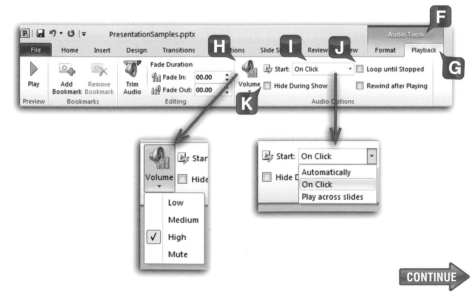

CONTINUE

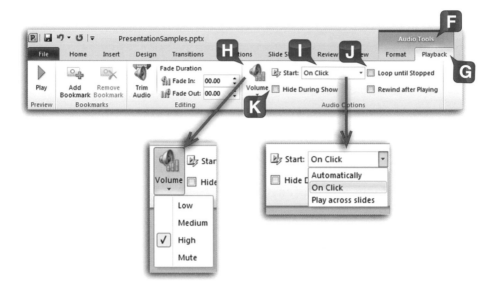

- **On Click** begins the audio when the audio controls bar is clicked.

  » **Automatically**: begins the audio as soon as the slide is opened.

  » **Play across slides** will continue playing the music even when you move through the next slides. This feature creates a background music effect.

- **Loop until Stopped**: Click the **Loop Until Stopped** checkbox **J** to tell PowerPoint to repeat an audio clip continuously until you stop the loop or you move to the next slide.

- **Hide During Show**: Click the **Hide During Show** **K** checkbox when you do not want the audio icon to be visible on your slides in **Slide Show** view.

Hot Tip: PowerPoint 2010 comes with many audio clips in the Clip Art Gallery. To quickly find audio clips, click the down arrow on the **Audio** combo button **F**, then choose **Clip Art Audio.** The **Clip Art** pane will open with **Audio** media types already filtered. Browse and search for a sound that will work for you, then select it to insert it into your slide.

Hot Tip: To specify when an audio clip will stop playing, click on the **Animations** tab and open the **Animations pane**. Look for the audio event in the list, select it, and open the dropdown menu. Select **Effect Options** **G** to open the **Play Audio** dialog box. Choose how you want your audio to end by choosing your settings in the **Stop Playing** section **H**.

STOP

Insert Audio into a Slide　　69

25 | Add a Picture or Graphic to Your Presentation

Difficulty: ●○○○

PROBLEM You are creating a slide show of properties that your real estate agency represents to run in the lobby of your offices. You would like to include photos of the houses and buildings in addition to addresses and property information.

SOLUTION Adding images into a slide is an easy way to add a visual element to your presentation. PowerPoint offers a robust set of tools for inserting and editing images so you can get the most out of your presentations. You can use your images to enhance text, fill shapes, and create interesting slide backgrounds.

Step-by-Step

Insert an Image

1. Position the cursor where the image should be placed.

2. On the **Insert** tab in the **Images** group, click the **Picture** button  to open the **Insert Picture** dialog box.

3. Browse for and select the filename of your image, then click the **Insert** button **B** to insert the image into the presentation.

Step-by-Step

Insert Clip Art

1. Position the cursor where the **Clip Art** should be placed.

2. On the **Insert** tab in the **Images** group, select the **Clip Art** button **C** to open the **Clip Art** task pane.

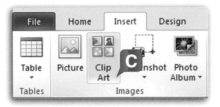

3. In the **Search for:** text box **D**, type a keyword to find the kind of picture you are looking for then click the **Go** button to find clip art results that match your keyword. 🌢

4. Click on the image you want to insert into your document. Click the **Close** button **E** on the task pane when you are done inserting **Clip Art**. 🌢

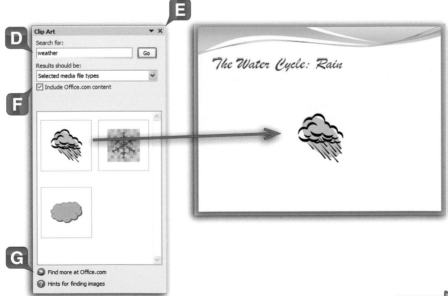

CONTINUE

Hot Tip: For more **Clip Art** selections, click the **Include Office.com** content checkbox **F** to gain access to all the **Clip Art** available on Office.com. You will need an internet connection for this to work. Clicking on the **Find more at Office.com** link **G** at the bottom of the **Clip Art** task pane will open a browser window to Microsoft's complete online collection of art.

Bright Idea: Narrow your selection by using the **Results should be:** dropdown **H** in the **Clip Art** task pane. By checking only **Illustrations**, for example, you will only have to browse through art that is hand-drawn and more casual. If your document requires more formal or realistic images, click the **Photographs** option to view only photographic images. *See Also: Insert Audio into a Slide*

Bright Idea: Shrink your document's file size by compressing images and removing cropped area data. To compress images in your document, select any image and then click the **Compress Pictures** button in the **Adjust** group on the **Format** tab. You can choose to apply compression to just the selected image or to all images in the document.

Add a Picture or Graphic to Your Presentation   **73**

26 | Use an Image as a Slide Background

Difficulty: ●●○○

PROBLEM You are creating a slide show for your antique car club's monthly meeting. You would like to create slides that are visually interesting and fun for your members. You would also like to use images of some of the members' cars throughout the presentation.

SOLUTION Use a picture as a slide background. One great way to make a presentation more personal is to use images that are interesting to your specific audience rather than stock backgrounds. In the business community, many people are very familiar with all of PowerPoint's standard themes and backgrounds. Customizing a background with your own images or graphics can immediately create an impression of personalization and professionalism.

See Also: Change the Background

Step-by-Step

1. In the thumbnail pane, click the slide or slides that you want to display your background picture then click the **Design** tab.

2. To launch the **Format Background** dialog box, click the **Background Styles** button **A** on the **Background** group, then choose **Format Background** **B** from the dropdown menu. ✱

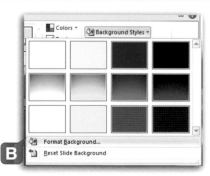

3. Click the **Fill** tab 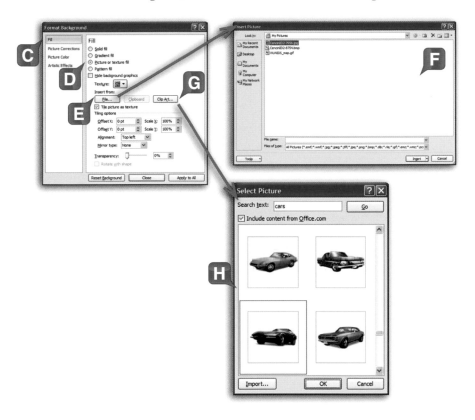, then click the **Picture or texture fill** radio button.

4. To insert a picture from a file on your hard drive or local network:
   - To select an image from your hard drive or local network, click the **File** button **E** under the **Insert from:** heading to open the **Insert Picture** dialog box.
   - If you would like to use a file from Microsoft Office's **Clip Art** gallery, click the **Clip Art** button **G** to open the **Insert Picture** dialog box.

5. Browse to the name of the file you want to insert and select it. Click **Insert** in the **Insert Picture** dialog box, or **OK** in the **Select Picture** dialog box.

6. Make adjustments to your background image such as alignment, transparency, and tiling preferences until you are happy with your background.

7. Click **Close** to apply the background only to the images you have selected, or click **Apply to All** to apply the background to all the slides in your presentation.

Hot Tip: Many of the picture editing tools are available in the **Format Background** dialog box. Adjust the color and contrast 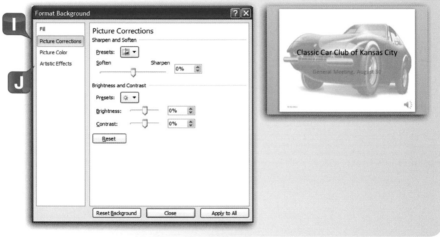 of your background image, or apply **Artistic Effects** directly from the dialog box. *See also: Edit an Image's Color*

Quickest Click: To quickly open the **Format Background** dialog box, click the dialog box launcher in the **Background** group on the **Design** tab.

27 | Stack and Group Images

Difficulty: ●●○○

PROBLEM You have a series of slides that you need to edit. Moving the images on those slides one at a time is proving to be a time-intensive task.

SOLUTION PowerPoint, by default, places each image separately within its own layer on the screen, allowing you to move each image individually without affecting any of the text or other images on the page. By grouping the images together, you can move multiple images at once. By changing the layer order, you can move objects behind and in front of each other.

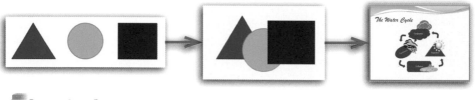

Step-by-Step

Re-Ordering Objects

1. Select the object to layer.

2. Click the **Format** tab **A** under **Drawing Tools** or **Picture Tools** contextual tabs, depending on what type of object your image is.

3. Click **Bring Forward** **B** or **Send Backward** **C** to move an object one position within the layers. By default, graphics are stacked in the order they are drawn.

4. To move an object all the way forward or all the way back, open the dropdown on the **Bring Forward** or **Send Backward** combo button.

5. Click either **Bring to Front** or **Send to Back**. ✦

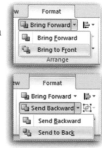

Step-by-Step

Group Shapes

1. Create a grouping by selecting all the pieces i.e. click and drag a box around the entire collection of shapes or click one item, and then hold the **CTRL** key as you click each additional item to add it to the selection.

2. Click the **Format** tab under **Drawing Tools** or **Picture Tools** contextual tabs, depending on what type of object your image is.

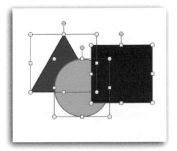

3. Click the **Group** button  D in the **Arrange** group to open the dropdown menu, then select **Group** E.

Individual selection handles disappear and a single set of selection handles **F** appears for the whole group. ✴

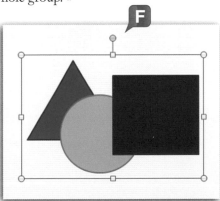

Step-by-Step

Ungroup Shapes

1. Select the grouped object you want to ungroup.

2. Click the **Format** tab under **Drawing Tools** or **Picture Tools** contextual tabs, and then click the **Group** button in the **Arrange** group.

3. Click **Ungroup** . Individual selection handles return for each object.

 Quickest Click: To re-order objects in layers, select your object then right-click. Select **Bring to Front** or **Send to Back** from the right-click fly-out menu and choose the option you need.

 Quickest Click: To group or ungroup shapes, select all the objects you want grouped, then right-click. Select **Group** from the fly-out menu and then choose the option you need.

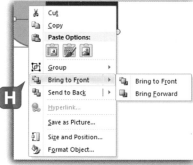

You can also access layering and grouping options on the **Home** tab in the **Drawing** group. Click the **Arrange** button  to open the dropdown menu. Select the order or grouping option needed.

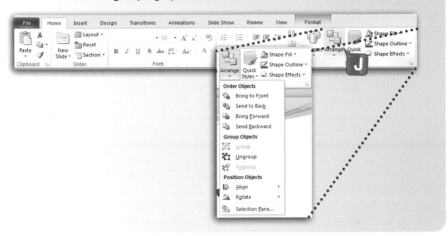

 Hot Tip: If you are having trouble selecting an object because it is hidden behind other objects, or because there are many objects on your slide, use the **Selection and Visibility** task pane to select and re-order objects.

1. On the **Home** tab in the **Drawing** group. Click the **Arrange** button **J** to open the drop-down menu. Click **Selection Pane** to open the **Selection and Visibility** task pane to view a list of all objects on your slide and the order they are layered in.

2. Select the object you want to adjust from the **Shapes on this Slide:** list, then click the up or down arrow at the bottom of the task pane to move the object up or down a layer at a time **K**.

28 Edit an Image's Color

Difficulty: ●●●○

PROBLEM You have just completed a PowerPoint presentation for the next manager's meeting when your boss informs you that your company's logo, which is featured prominently on several slides, has changed colors.

SOLUTION Use the Format Picture ribbon. By right-clicking on the image of your company's logo and selecting Format Picture from the drop-down menu, you can choose to edit several of your image's properties, such as size, position, and color.

Step-by-Step

Adjust Image Color

1. Click on the image you want to adjust. The **Picture Tools** contextual tab **A** will appear. Click the **Format** tab **B**.

2. In the **Adjust** group, select the **Color** button **C**. If the graphic is a photograph, the **Color** dropdown menu will allow you to edit **Color Saturation**, **Color Tone**, and give you **Recolor** options. *Note:* if the graphic is an illustration, you will only see the **Recolor** options.

   The image's current settings will be highlighted **D**. Your image will preview the selections when you hover over the options:

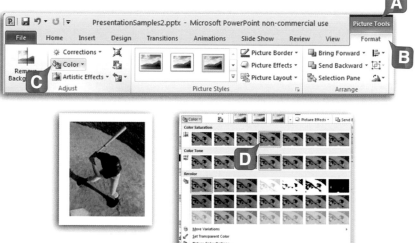

- **Color Saturation:** Saturation describes the intensity of the color in a photograph. A higher saturation will make a picture look more vivid and the colors brighter. A lower saturation shades the colors towards gray.

- **Color Tone:** Color Tone describes the dominant color influencing a picture. When a camera does not measure the color temperature correctly, for example, a picture can look too blue or too orange. The Color Tone allows you to adjust the color temperature to enhance picture details and make the picture look better. The higher the temperature, the more orange is added to your picture. The lower the temperature, the more blue is added.

- **Recolor:** Recolor gives you a set of built-in stylized effects. Some options, like grayscale or sepia, are common color changes. You can also choose to recolor your image based upon your document's theme, allowing you to match images or illustrations to your theme's color palette for a professional and consistent look.

Step-by-Step

Set Transparent Color

You may want to make part of your picture transparent to make it work better with text that is layered on top or beneath it. Transparent areas in a picture appear as the same color as the paper on which it is printed or the background on which it is displayed (as on a web site). Only one color per picture can be set to transparent in PowerPoint 2010.

1. Click on the image you want to adjust. The **Picture Tools** contextual tab **A** will appear. Click the **Format** tab **B**.

2. In the **Adjust** group, select the **Color** button **C** to open the **Picture Color** dropdown menu. Click **Set Transparent Color** menu option **E**.

3. Your cursor will turn to a color selection tool **F**. Click the color in the picture or illustration that you want to make transparent. ⚠

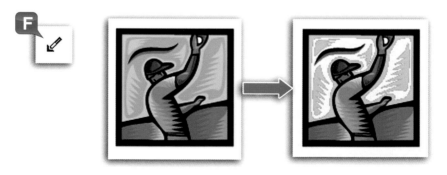

Caution: If the picture you are using varies widely in color (such as a photograph of the sunset), this option will not be as useful. The transparency tool is most useful in an image with solid color backgrounds.

 Hot Tip: For even more artistic options, click on the **Artistic Effects** button **G** in the **Adjust** group of the **Format** tab. From here, you can choose effects like **Pencil Sketch**, **Cement**, **Glow Edges**, and more that will change your photograph's look and design.

Hot Tip: Many of these editing tools are available to you from the **Format Background** dialog box. If you are using a photographic image for your slide background, use these editing tools to adjust the image as you are setting up your slides.

29 | Crop and Resize Images

Difficulty: ●●○○

PROBLEM The art department for your advertising company has provided you with an image file of your client's logo to be featured in your upcoming presentation for them. The image, when placed on a PowerPoint slide, is far too large and obscures the text.

SOLUTION Use the **Format Picture** ribbon. By right-clicking on the image that you have placed on the slide, and selecting **Format Picture** from the dropdown menu, you can choose to move the image to a new location, crop the image, or resize it to better fit the slide.

Step-by-Step

Crop, Resize, or Rotate an Image

1. Click on the image you want to adjust. The **Picture Tools** contextual tab **A** will appear. Click the **Format** tab **B**.

- To resize the image, click the up or down arrows in the **Height C** or **Width D** boxes in the **Size** group, or type in the specific measurements you want. By default, the aspect ratio will be locked, and the shape will expand or shrink in proportion to its original size.

- To rotate your image, click the **Rotate** button **E** in the **Arrange** group on the **Format** tab. Choose a rotation direction or flip option from the dropdown menu. Your slide will perform the rotation for you to preview when you hover over the menu options.

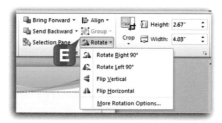

- For more resizing and rotation options, click on **More Rotation Options** F in the **Rotate** dropdown menu or the dialog box launcher on the **Size** group G to open the **Format Picture** dialog box.

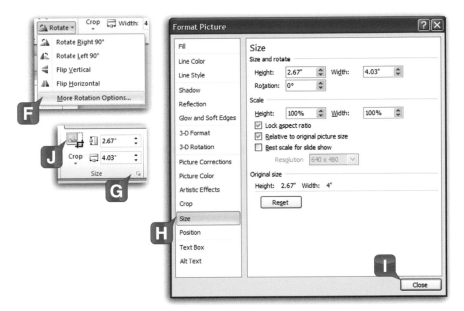

CONTINUE

- On the **Size** tab 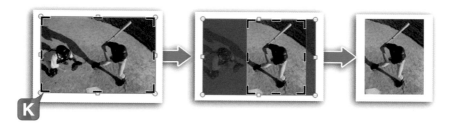 in the **Format Picture** dialog box, make the changes you want to adjust your images, size or rotation. This is also where you can unlock the aspect ratio and adjust size by percentage. Click **Close** to apply your changes.

- To crop the image, click the **Crop** button in the **Size** group on the **Format** tab. Black line **handles** will be added to the image. Click and drag the handles to trim unneeded edges of your image. When you click away from the image, the cropped sections will disappear. Click **Crop** again to see the complete image.

Quickest Click: You can resize and rotate a shape manually by clicking and dragging any of the **size handles**  that appear when an object is selected. The long, green handle allows you to rotate the image.

Quickest Click: Many of the above features are available at a click. **Crop, Rotate, Height, Width, Bring Forward,** and **Send Backward** menus are also available in the right-click fly-out menu **M**.

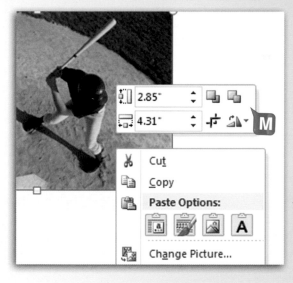

30 | Add Style to Images

Difficulty: ●●○○

PROBLEM The images you have chosen to use for your upcoming presentation look a little bland, and you want them to compliment the text in a more appealing way.

SOLUTION Use the Format Picture ribbon. To make your images stand out or to help your images illustrate your text in a visually appealing way, you can add style elements to the image directly from PowerPoint. Styles available include adding a border to your image, tilting the image at a 45-degree angle, adding 3-D effects, and changing the shape of your image.

 Step-by-Step

Add a Quick Style

1. Click on the image you want to adjust. The **Picture Tools** contextual tab **A** will appear. Click the **Format** tab **B**.

2. In the **Picture Styles** group, select the **More** button **C** in the **Quick Styles** selection box to open the **Quick Styles** dropdown menu **D**.

3. Choose from the options that consist of common border and effects combinations. Your image will change for you to preview the selection when you hover over the choices. Click your choice to apply the style.

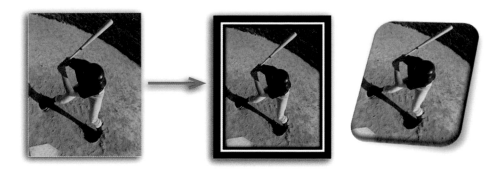

Step-by-Step

Create Your Own Styles

1. Click on the image you want to enhance. The **Picture Tools** contextual tab **A** will appear. Click the **Format** tab **B**.

    • To add a border to your image, click the **Picture Border** button **E** in the **Picture Styles** group. Select a color for your border from the **Theme Color** palette **F**. Choose the thickness of your border from the **Line Weight** fly-out menu **G**. Your image will change for you to preview the selection when you hover over the choices. Click your choice to apply the style.

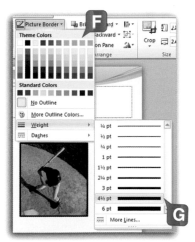

CONTINUE

- To add an effect to your image, click the **Picture Effects** button 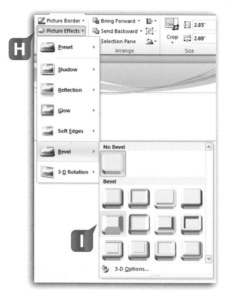 in the **Picture Styles** group. Select an effect for your image from the **Picture Effects** dropdown menus . Your image will change for you to preview the selection when you hover over the choices. Click your choice to apply the style.

Hot Tip: For even more control over effects, click on the **Format Picture** dialog box launcher **J** *or* any **Options** link **K** at the bottom of each effects pop-out menu to launch the **Format Picture** dialog box.

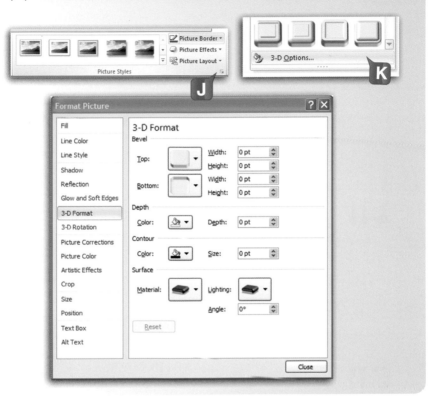

31 | Remove the Background from an Image

Difficulty: ●●●●

PROBLEM You have a candid picture of a guest speaker that you would like to use in the publicity letters you are preparing for an event. The picture of the speaker is very good, but the background colors clash with your theme and don't fit the style of your overall look. You would like a way just to use the main, foreground image.

SOLUTION Remove the background from the image. Microsoft introduced advanced picture editing options in the 2010 version of PowerPoint to give you even better control over the images you use in your documents without purchasing a high-end image editor. The automatic background removal tool will select the object in the foreground of your image and remove all parts of the background that you don't want. With this tool, you can produce appealing images that are more interesting than the usual rectangle.

> **What Microsoft Calls It:** Automatic Background Removal

Step-by-Step

1. Click on the image you want to adjust. The **Picture Tools** contextual tab **A** will appear. Click the **Format** tab **B**.

2. Click the **Background Removal** button **C** in the **Adjust** group.

A marquee box **D** will appear in your image, and the **Background Removal** contextual tab will open. The background removal tool will make its best guess as to what you want to keep. Everything that the tool plans to remove will be shaded purple **E**.

3. Click the handles on the marquee box and drag the lines so that everything you want to keep is included, but the majority of the rest of the background is outside. Adjust the marquee until the image you want to retain is properly highlighted. ⚠

4. If you cannot get the marquee box to select the results you want, do one or both of the following:

    • Click **Mark Areas to Keep** **F** to manually indicate the parts of the picture that should remain in the final version.

    • Click **Mark Areas to Remove** **G** to manually indicate the parts of the picture that are background and should be removed.

    • Click **Delete Mark** **H** if you need to change either of the above marks after you have made them.

5. When the image is marked as needed and the background is correctly shaded
    I, click **Keep Changes** **J** in the **Close** group to apply the background
    removal. If you decide to cancel the automatic background removal, click
    Discard All Changes.

Bright Idea: Once the background has been removed from an image, you
can add effects such as shadows, reflections, and glows.

Hot Tip: It is a good idea to compress and save a picture before you remove the background since compressing can change the amount of detail stored in the source picture.

Caution: Make sure the highlighted regions are accurate, or the automatic background removal tool will leave pieces of your image you don't want and remove pieces that you do.

32 | Add a Screenshot to Your Presentation

Difficulty: ●●●○

PROBLEM You are preparing a pitch to potential clients featuring the newest version of your company's accounting software. It would be an incredible selling tool to be able to include screenshots from the software in your presentation.

SOLUTION Inserting a screenshot is a simple process in Microsoft PowerPoint. You can capture all, or part, of an available window to include on your slide without installing separate screen capturing software or even leaving PowerPoint.

Step-by-Step

Insert an Entire Program Window

1. Click on the slide that you want the screenshot added to, then click the **Insert** tab.

2. Click the **Screenshot** button **A** in the **Images** group to open the **Available Windows** dropdown menu.

3. Click on the window you want to capture as a screenshot **B** to apply the screenshot as an image to your slide **C**. Adjust the image size and placement as needed. *See Also: Crop and Resize Images*

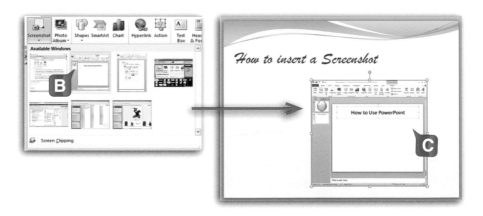

Step-by-Step

Insert a Screen Clipping

1. Arrange your windows so that the one you want to capture a clipping of is directly below the PowerPoint window you are working on.

2. Click on the slide that you want the screenshot added to, then click the **Insert** tab.

3. Click the **Screenshot** button **A** in the **Images** group to open the **Available Windows** dropdown menu.

4. Click the **Screen Clipping** menu option **D** at the bottom of the **Available Windows** menu. Your pointer will become a cross **E**.

5. Hold the left mouse button and drag to select the area of the screen that you want in your screenshot. Release the mouse when your selection is complete to apply the screenshot as an image to your slide **F**. Adjust the image size and placement as needed. *See Also: Crop and Resize Images*

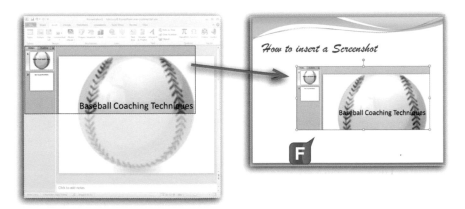

STOP

33 | Insert a SmartArt Graphic

Difficulty: ●○○○

PROBLEM You need to explain the changes you have made to your client's corporate org chart. You want a way to show the complex relationships between management levels and explain how employees will report up the management chain. You have a spreadsheet with employee names and titles in the new structure, but you would like a quick, simple way to give your client a big-picture view before you discuss details.

SOLUTION Use SmartArt graphics. Data can be compelling information, but often you need to express the numbers graphically to help others understand what they mean. Charts and process maps created with the powerful SmartArt tool provide visually appealing, dynamic images to convey information clearly. SmartArt graphics are divided into seven categories. Some graphics can be used to express multiple concepts and so appear in more than one category. Here is a list of the categories and an explanation for each:

All: This is not a category. By choosing this option, you can view all graphics from all categories.

List: These graphics are best used to express static lists of information.

Process: These graphics are best used to express processes and procedures where there are multiple steps with various effects, consequences, and paths.

Cycle: These graphics are best used to express cyclical events or repetitive processes.

Hierarchy: These graphics are best used to display groups or lists where one item takes precedence over another.

Relationship: These graphics are best used to display information that is connected to or dependent on other information, resources, or processes.

Matrix: These graphics are best used to show the relationship of information or components to a whole.

Pyramid: These graphics combine hierarchy and relationship. Higher levels depend on the items in the levels below.

Step-by-Step

1. Click the **SmartArt** button **A** in the **Illustrations** group of the **Insert** tab to open the **Choose a SmartArt Graphic** dialog box.

2. In the **Choose a SmartArt Graphic** dialog box, select a **SmartArt** category from the left panel **B** to reveal the graphic options for that category in the center panel **C**.

3. Click a graphic to reveal a sample of what it will look like once it is inserted in the right panel **D**. This panel also includes a brief description of the graphic and the information it would best be used to convey **E**.

4. When you have found the graphic you want to insert, make sure it is selected and then click the **OK** button.

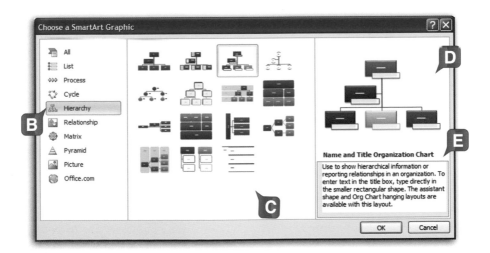

34 | Configure a SmartArt Graphic

Difficulty: ●●○○

PROBLEM You have added a SmartArt image to your slide, and you want to change the default colors and fonts into something more suitable for your presentation.

SOLUTION Once you have added a SmartArt image to your presentation, two new tabs will appear on the Ribbon: the SmartArt design tab and the SmartArt format tab. From these two tabs, you can change many of the parameters of the default SmartArt object.

Step-by-Step

Configure a SmartArt Graphic

1. Select the graphic so it is active. You can tell a graphic is selected or active if you can see the border around the items **A**.

2. Select an area marked **[Text]** and begin typing to enter your information directly into the graphic **B**. You can also expand the text pane **C** by clicking the control tab on the SmartArt border **D**. Type your text beside the bullets. Use tabs to add sub-levels of hierarchy.

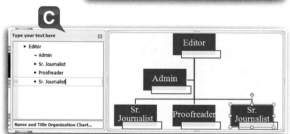

3. Once you have entered all of your text elements, use the tools on the **SmartArt Tools Design** and **SmartArt Tools Format** tabs to adjust the appearance of your graphic.

Design Tab:

- **Create Graphic Group:** Here you can insert additional items (the **Add Bullet** button), elements (the **Add Shape** button), or adjust the direction of the graphic **E**.
- **Layouts Group:** In this section you can adjust the entire graphic **F**.

- **SmartArt Styles Group:** These tools let you change the look and feel of your graphic (borders, drop shadows, rotation, reflection, etc.) **G**.

- **Reset:** This button returns the graphic to its original state before you started making adjustments **H**.

Format Tab:

- **Shapes:** These tools let you select an element or group of elements in your graphic and change their shape. In the example at right, you could change the rectangles containing text to a different shape **N** based on job description **I**.

- **Shape Styles:** Here you can adjust the look and feel of an element or group of elements. In the example at right, you could change the style from a white outline with blue fill to a blue outline with a white fill **O**. **J**

- **WordArt Styles:** Most SmartArt graphic text is displayed in WordArt. As a result, you can change the appearance of the text with many settings, including color, outline, shadow, 3D, and more **K**.

- **Arrange:** This button gives you access to change the arrangement of the elements within your SmartArt graphic and the arrangement of multiple graphics on the page (if you have more than one) **L**.

- **Size:** This button gives you access to tools that will allow you to change the physical (print) size of the SmartArt graphic **M**.

35 | Add a Shape to Your Slide

Difficulty: ●○○○

PROBLEM Your kindergarten class is learning about shapes and colors. As part of your interactive presentation for the students to use, you'd like to include shapes for them to identify.

SOLUTION Insert a shape. PowerPoint offers a large collection of standard and business-targeted shapes to add interest to your presentation. By combining arrows, rectangles, callouts, and banner figures, you can create complex diagrams and illustrations to enhance your text.

Step-by-Step

Insert a Shape

1. Position the cursor where the shape should be placed.

2. On the **Insert** tab, in the **Images** group, click the **Shapes** button **A** to open the **shapes** dropdown menu.

3. Click on the shape that you want to add to your slide from the menu.

4. Your cursor will change to a plus sign **B**. Click in the slide and drag to draw the shape to the size you want **C**. Adjust the image size and placement as needed. *See Also: Crop and Resize Images; Configure a SmartArt Graphic*

36 | Import Data from an Excel Spreadsheet into a Document

Difficulty: ●●●○

PROBLEM As part of your upcoming investor's conference, you are giving a presentation on the company's fiscal results. Typing the data from your Excel spreadsheet would be time-consuming and difficult. You would like to simply reuse the data and charts you have already created in Microsoft Excel in your slides.

SOLUTION Import your data from Microsoft Excel. With PowerPoint's Insert Object feature, you can either copy your data from a spreadsheet, or create a link to your data so that your presentation will stay up-to-date when changes are made at the source. In both cases, PowerPoint allows you to easily format the data into your current theme styles.

Step-by-Step

Insert an Excel Object

1. Place your cursor at the point where the Excel spreadsheet will be inserted.

2. On the **Insert** tab, in the **Text** group, click the **Object** button  to open the **Insert Object** dialog box.

3. Click the **Create from File** tab **B**.

4. Click **Browse** **C** to select the location and select the file to include in the document.

   • To link to an object, click the **Link** checkbox **D**. A linked object will be updated if the original is changed. This is very useful if you re-use the slide or repeat your presentation frequently. With a linked object, you will only have to update the data in the source, and the presentation will automatically reflect those changes. ⚠

   • To embed the source data, simply make sure the **Link** checkbox is unchecked. Your source data will become part of the PowerPoint presentation.

- To add only an icon  E that will open your spreadsheet when you click on it from the slide, check the **Display as icon** checkbox **F**.

5. Click **OK**.

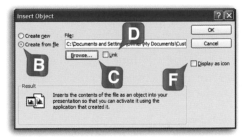

Caution: Your source file must be available on your local hard drive or network for PowerPoint to properly display a linked object. Be sure that you move linked source content with your presentation.

Bright Idea: You can insert a blank Excel spreadsheet into an existing PowerPoint presentation. This allows for data manipulation that a PowerPoint table does not allow, such as flexibility in sorting, formatting, and formulas/functions. On the **Insert** tab, in the **Text** group, select **Object**. With the **Create New** radio button selected, select an Excel spreadsheet format from the **Object type:** menu. Click **OK**.

Double-click any Excel spreadsheet object to edit its contents.

37 | Insert a Hyperlink into a Presentation

Difficulty: ●●●○

PROBLEM You have a self-running kiosk in a popular shopping mall. You need a way for those viewing the presentation to not only move from slide to slide, but also to send an e-mail to your sales department when they type in their information.

SOLUTION A hyperlink can connect from slide to slide within the same presentation, to a slide in another presentation, and to link to an e-mail address, a web page or a file. You can hyperlink an object, picture, graph, shape, or WordArt.

Step-by-Step

1. Select the text or the image that will be formatted as a hyperlink.

2. On the **Insert** tab in the **Links** group, click **Hyperlink** **A** to open the **Insert Hyperlink** dialog box. ✸

3. Select the **Link to:** location:

   • **Existing File or Web Page** **B**: Select this option if you want to link to another PowerPoint document on your computer or the network, or if you want to link to a web page.

   • **To link to a document:** Browse your computer or the network for a document you want to link. The **Look in:** dropdown **C** displays the folder you are currently viewing. Double-click the document you want to link to. The **Insert Hyperlink** box closes and PowerPoint creates the link.

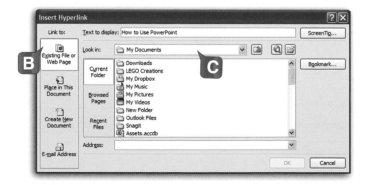

- **To link to a Web page**: Click the **Browse the Web** icon in the upper-right corner **D** to open your default web browser. Go to the web page you want to link to and then go back to the **Insert Hyperlink** dialog box. PowerPoint adds the

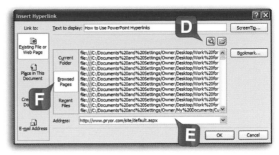

address in your web browser to the **Address** text box **E**. To see links to Web pages you have recently visited, click the **Browsed Pages** button **F**. Click any of these URLs to add it to the **Address** text box.

- **Place in This Document** **G**: Select this option if you are creating a link to jump around in a long presentation. PowerPoint can create links to either specific slides or custom shows. *See Also: Create Navigation Buttons to Advance Your Presentation*

- **Create New Document** **H**: Select this option to create a hyperlink to a document you have not created yet. Type the name of the new document you want to create in the **Name of new document:** text box **I**. Click **OK** to save your new document.

- **E-mail Address** **J**: Select this option to create a mail-to hyperlink in your document. Type the e-mail address that you want hyperlinked in the **E-mail address:** text box **K**, then type the subject text you would like added to the subject line if you wish **L**.

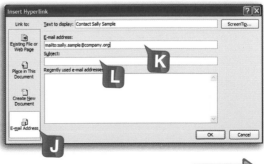

CONTINUE

4. Click the **ScreenTip** button to open the **Set Hyperlink Screen Tip** dialog box and add a screen tip to the hyperlink. This is text that appears in a box when the user hovers over the hyperlink within a web browser. This text is optional.

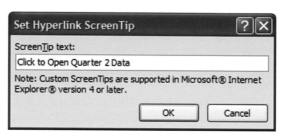

5. **The Text to display:** text box 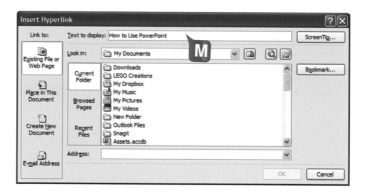 is where you edit the text that is hyperlinked. For example, if you want to have users click on the words "Click here" instead of the name of the presentation, you can edit the text in the **Text to display:** box and PowerPoint will display this text in the presentation once you click **OK**. ⚠

6. When edits are complete, click **OK** to apply.

7. The text you highlighted is now blue and underlined, indicating that it is an active hyperlink.

8. Users can **CTRL+click** on the hyperlink to follow the link.

Quickest Click: Select the text to be linked, then right-click and select **Hyperlink** from the menu.

Caution: If you edit the text in the **Text to Display** box, make sure that the text you've entered fits within the context of your slide. You may have to go back into your presentation and review/edit to verify.

38 | Record a Narration

Difficulty:

PROBLEM As part of an interactive presentation for the museum where you work, you have prepared a slide show of beautiful images of your exhibits. However, there is not enough room to display all the text that would be required to explain the images in detail, and so much written information would be overwhelming or boring. You need a better way to deliver this important information.

SOLUTION Record a narration. Narration is an excellent way to give those viewing your presentation a large amount of information without having to add a lot of text to a slide. An audio element in your presentation can add interest without creating visual clutter.

Step-by-Step

1. Open the presentation file you want to narrate, then click on the **Slide Show** tab.

2. In the **Set Up** group, click the down arrow on the **Record Slide Show** combo button **A**. Choose **Start Recording from Beginning** or **Start Recording from Current Slide** to open the **Record Slide Show** dialog box.

3. If you want **Record Slide Show** to record the timings between slides, check the **Slide and animation** timings checkbox **B**. If you want to record the motion of the laser pointer as you narrate, check the **Narrations and laser pointer** checkbox **C**.

4. When you are ready to begin your narration, click **Start Recording** **D**.

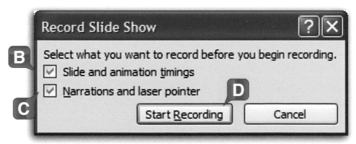

- Your slide show will begin and the **Recording** pane will appear. Speak into your microphone to record your narration. The middle clock on the **Recording** pane  E keeps track of the time you have spent on the current slide. The rightmost clock F keeps track of the total presentation time.

- Advance your slides and animations by clicking on the screen or by clicking the **Next** button G on the **Recording** menu.

- To pause the recording, click the **Pause** button H on the **Recording** menu. To begin recording again, click the **Resume Recording** button in the message box.

- To repeat a recording for the current slide, click the **Repeat** button I to start that slide, and your narration, from the beginning.

5. Your recording will stop when you have reached the end of your presentation or when you right-click a slide and select **End Show** J from the fly-out menu.

6. Your recorded slide show timings (if you recorded them) will display in the **Slide Sorter** view beneath each slide **K**. A sound icon **L** will appear in the bottom right corner of all slides that have a recorded narration.

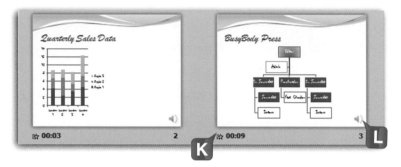

- To preview your narration, click on the sound icon in **Normal View**, then click the **Preview** button **M** on the **Playback** contextual tab.

- To delete a narration or timings from a single slide or all slides, click the down arrow on the **Record Slide Show** combo button. Click **Clear** **N**, then select the menu option that you need.

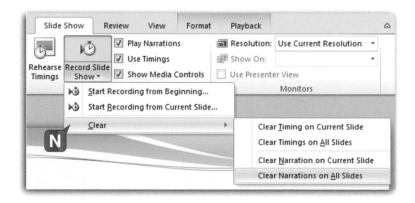

Caution: Make sure your microphone and sound card are correctly installed and plugged in before you try to record a narration. Test your equipment on the first slide or two, then preview to make sure everything is working as you expect.

39 | Create a Photo Album

Difficulty: ●●○○

PROBLEM To celebrate your parents' 50th wedding anniversary, you want to take old photos of your parents together over the years and create a slide show to play during their anniversary party.

SOLUTION Microsoft PowerPoint contains a built-in Photo Album feature. The Photo Album dialog box offers a convenient way to insert and organize lots of images into pre-set album formatting. With the Photo Album dialog box, you can choose album layout, theme and image styles; edit and crop your images; and add captions.

Step-by-Step

Create a New Album and Insert Images

1. Open a new PowerPoint presentation, then click the **Insert** tab.

2. In the **Images** group, click the **Photo Album A** combo button to launch the **Photo Album** dialog box.

3. To insert a picture, click the **File/Disk** button **B** under the **Insert picture from:** heading to open the **Insert New Pictures** dialog box.

4. Browse to the folder where your pictures are stored and click on the image **C** you want to add to your album. **SHIFT+click** or drag your mouse to add multiple images at once.

5. Click **Insert D**.

Your image files will be added to the **Pictures in album:** pane **E** in the **Photo Album** dialog box and a preview of each image is shown in the **Preview:** pane **F**.

6. Choose a picture layout style for your album by opening the **Picture layout:** dropdown menu **G** under the **Album Layout** heading. If you choose to show more than one picture per slide, choose the style of frame you want for the pictures from the **Frame shape:** dropdown menu **H**.

   Choose a theme for your album by clicking on the **Browse** button beside the **Theme:** textbox **I**. Select the theme you want, then click **Select**.

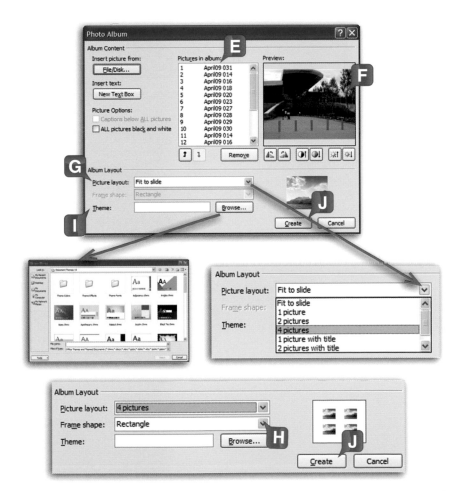

7. Click the **Create** button  to create your album and apply your layout style and theme.

Hot Tip: You can edit the colors and appearance of your images in your album. In the **Images** group on the **Insert** tab, click the down arrow on the **Photo Album** button, then click **Edit Photo Album** to open the **Edit Photo Album** dialog box.

Select the image (or images) you want to edit, then use the edit options **K** underneath the **Preview:** window to make your adjustments. *See also: Edit an Image's Color; Crop and Resize Images*

Bright Idea: Add captions to your album so your audience can quickly learn more about your pictures while they are watching the slide show. In the **Images** group on the **Insert** tab, click the down arrow on the **Photo Album** button, then click **Edit Photo Album** to open the **Edit Photo Album** dialog box.

Click the **Captions below ALL pictures** checkbox, then click **Update**. A caption text box will be added below every image. Click in the caption text box in Normal View and replace the (default) image's file name with your own text.

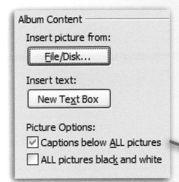

April09 Soldier Field, Chicago, IL1

40 | Play Your Slide Show in Presenter View

Difficulty: ●●○○

PROBLEM Having given several successful presentations for your company in the past, you are selected to present your newest product at an upcoming trade show. Since this will be a live presentation, you want control over which slides are shown and in what order, and you want to see your notes while the slide show is running.

SOLUTION Use Presenter View. PowerPoint offers options that allow you more control over your slide show, such as the ability to show slides out of sequence, choose which slides are shown in real-time, and to include a black out button that allows you to darken the screen for the audience while still showing the presentation and your notes on your own computer. Presenter View allows you to run your presentation from one monitor and let the audience view it on another monitor or a projector.

Your computer must support use of multiple monitors to use Presenter View.

Step-by-Step

1. Open the presentation you are ready to run, then click the **Slide Show** tab.

2. Click the **Set Up Slide Show** button **A** in the **Set Up group** to open the **Set Up Show** dialog box.

3. Select the **Presented by a speaker** radio button **B** under the **Show type** heading.

4. Under the **Multiple monitors** heading, click the **Show Presenter View** check box **C**, then choose the monitor that the slide show will be sent to from the **Display slide show on:** list **D**.

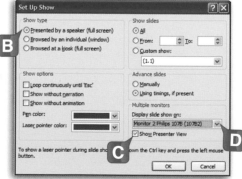

5. Click **OK**.

6. Click the **From Beginning** button  in the **Start Slide Show** group to begin your slide show in **Presenter View**.

One monitor will display the slide show as you have seen it previewed. The second monitor will display a set of tools just for the presenter to view and use to help deliver the presentation:

*   The slide that is currently being shown to the audience appears in the main pane **F**. Below the slide pane, the slide number, the elapsed presentation time; and current time are displayed.

*   Notes that have been added to the slide appear in the notes pane **G**. The speaker can expand or shrink the text using the zoom buttons below the notes pane **H**.

*   A bar of slide thumbnails lies across the bottom of the presenter view. The presenter can scroll through the entire presentation without disturbing the audience view, and can click on any thumbnail to send it to the display view.

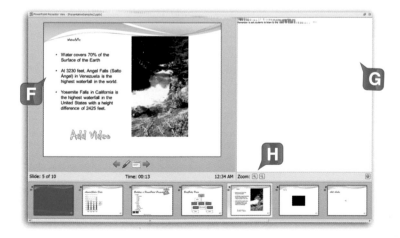

- Underneath the main slide pane are **Previous** 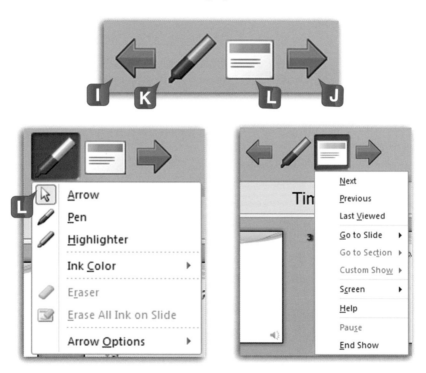 and **Next** buttons.
- The pen or highlighter icon lets the presenter "mark" on the slides to point out items to the audience. Right-click on the pen to change the style of the pointer and drawing tool.
- The **Slide Show** button opens a menu with options such as **End Show**, go to **Last Viewed**, and **Screen** setting options.

41 | Create Handouts

Difficulty: ●●○○

PROBLEM As part of an interactive presentation for a museum, you want to create handouts that follow along with the slides and that visitors can look at while your presentation is playing.

SOLUTION Create Handouts of your presentation. With the handout feature in PowerPoint, you can choose to print a single slide on a page or up to nine slides at a time per page. Handouts will include lined space by default for note taking.

Step-by-Step

Print Your Handouts from PowerPoint

1. Click the **File** tab, then select the **Print** tab **A**.

2. Under the **Settings** heading, choose a handout format **B** under the **Handouts** heading in the format dropdown menu. Make other settings changes as needed, such as number of copies and collation options. Preview your choices in the **Preview** pane **C**.

3. When you are ready to print, click the **Print** button **D** to send your handouts to the printer you have selected under the **Printer** heading **E**.

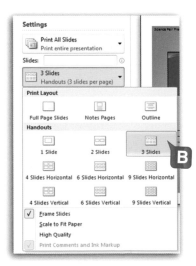

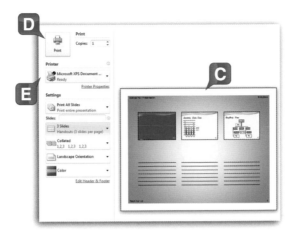

Step-by-Step

Edit Your Handouts in Microsoft Word

Sometimes you want to create more elaborate handouts than PowerPoint can provide. Microsoft gives you a way to easily export the handout template to Word where you can use Word's powerful editing and formatting features to create exactly what you need.

1. Open the **File** tab, then click **Save & Send F**.

2. Under the **File types** heading, click **Create Handouts G**.

3. In the rightmost pane, click the **Create Handouts** button **H** under the **Create Handouts in Microsoft Word** heading to open the **Send to Microsoft Word** dialog box.

4. Select the Handout style you want to export under the **Page layout in Microsoft Word** heading 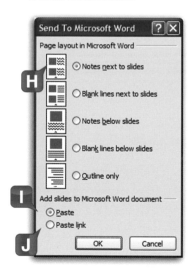.

5. Choose whether you would like to paste copies of the current versions of your slides into the new document, or if you would like to create a link to your slides from the new document under **Add slides to Microsoft Word document**.

   • Click the **Paste** radio button ⬛ to paste current versions of your slides. Your handouts will remain unchanged when you edit your PowerPoint presentation.

   • Click the **Paste link** radio button ⬛ to create a link between your PowerPoint presentation and Word document. This will allow Word to update any changes you make in your presentation and reflect them in your handouts.

6. Click **OK**. Microsoft Word will launch a new document ⬛ with your slides and notes lines. Make your edits as needed, then save and print your handouts per Word's instructions.

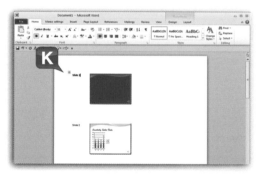

Caution: For slides and handouts that are to be printed, it is best to choose a theme with a white background and dark text. Light text on a dark background is difficult to read in print and wastes ink.

42 Package Your Presentation for CD

Difficulty: ●●○○

PROBLEM You have been assigned to design a presentation for a coworker to take on an upcoming business trip. Rather than run the presentation directly from the coworker's computer, you want to put it on a CD, for ease of use.

SOLUTION Microsoft PowerPoint supports running a presentation from a variety of formats, such as a PC, a CD, or a DVD. Creating a CD of your presentations lets you easily move them from venue to venue. When you use the **Package Presentation for CD** tool, it automatically finds and includes any linked files that the presentation uses, ensuring that all your data is where it should be.

Step-by-Step

1. Open the presentation that you want to copy onto a CD.

2. Click the **File** tab, then click the **Save & Send** tab **A**.

3. Under the **File Types** heading, click the **Package Presentation for CD** option **B**, then click the **Package for CD** button **C** that opens in the right pane to open the **Package for CD** dialog box.

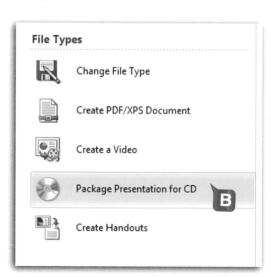

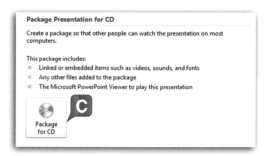

4. The presentation that you have open will automatically appear in the **Files to be copied** list **D**. To add more presentations to your CD, click the **Add** button **E**, then browse for the file you want, then click **Add**.

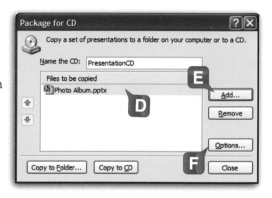

5. Click the **Options** button **F** to open the **Options** dialog box. Make sure that the **Linked files** checkbox **G** is checked.

    If you want to add password protection to your file, type your password in the **Password to open each presentation:** text box. This will prompt a viewer for the password before opening each file on the CD. Typing a password into the **Password to modify each presentation:** text box will prompt the user for a password when they attempt to make edits. Click **OK**.

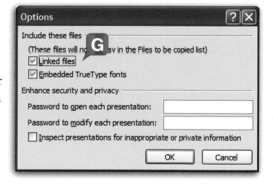

6. Click **Copy to CD**.

43 Create a Presentation to Run at a Kiosk

Difficulty: ●○○○

PROBLEM You have been given the opportunity to place a kiosk inside a popular attraction. The presentation will inform the public about the products and services that your company offers. You can't spare an employee to constantly monitor the kiosk and re-start the presentation from the beginning when it reaches the end.

SOLUTION Create a self-running Show. You can choose which elements to include and 6uhow much control to give users through the use of hyperlinks, add voice narration, and set up a form for users to enter their information.

 Step-by-Step

Design Your Presentation

Since you are planning for your presentation to run unattended, your slides must be set up in some specific ways that will work well for kiosk delivery:

- Slides can advance in one of only two ways in a self-running presentation: automatic timings or triggers and action buttons. Make sure that the **After:** checkbox **A** is checked in the **Timing** group on the **Transitions** tab and the number of seconds you want a slide to show **B** is added. If your kiosk offers the ability for viewers to interact with the presentation, make sure there are action buttons that advance the show **C**.

See Also: Create a Slide Transition; Create Navigation Buttons to Advance Your Presentation; Create an Interactive Activity; Set a Trigger on a Video or Audio Bookmark; Insert a Hyperlink into a Presentation

- Since you will not be speaking along with the presentation, audio clips and voice-over narration can cover the information you would normally perform personally. Video clips can create interest and add visual appeal to your information. *See also: Record a Narration; Insert Audio into a Slide; Add a Video to a Presentation*

 **Step-by-Step**

Set Up Show for Kiosk Delivery

Once your presentation is ready, you will need to set up your slide show with the proper settings:

1. In the **Set Up** group on the **Slide Show** tab, click the **Set Up Slide Show** button **D** to open the **Set Up Show** dialog box.

2. Choose the settings for kiosk delivery:
    - Click **Browsed at a kiosk** radio button **E**. The **Loop continuously until 'Esc'** checkbox will be automatically selected and the presentation will restart after it has reached the end or when the show has been idle for longer than five minutes.
    - Under **Advance** slides, make sure the **Using timings, if present** radio button **F** is selected.
    - Click **OK** to apply your settings to the slide show.

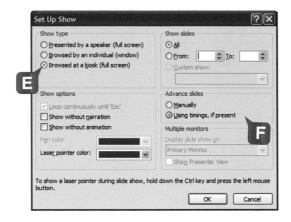

See Also: Set Up Show

Step-by-Step

Save Your Show File

Once you are happy with your animations, timings, and triggers, you need to save the presentation as a **Show File**. This will embed all sound and music files into the presentation so they will be included when you move the show between computers or email it to someone else.

5. Click on the **File** tab, then click **Save As** to open the **Save As** dialog box.

6. Type a name for your show in the **File Name:** text box.

7. Choose **PowerPointShow (*.ppsx)** from the **Save as type:** dropdown menu.

8. Click **Save**.

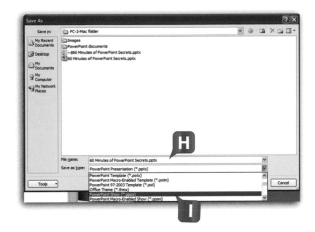

44 | Deliver a Presentation over the Internet

Difficulty: ●●○○

PROBLEM You are in charge of delivering a presentation to the various regional vice presidents of your company. Due to the travel costs and difficulty of having the VPs all meet in a central location, you want to deliver the presentation over the internet to each VP's office.

SOLUTION Broadcasting a presentation over the internet is a built-in feature of Microsoft PowerPoint. You can give your presentation remotely rather than having to gather an audience at the same location and at the same time. The Broadcast Slide Show feature contains the options that will allow you to broadcast your presentation over the internet.

To use the broadcast features, you will need a Windows Live ID (or an internal broadcast service). To sign up for Windows Live, go to *https://signup.live.com* and fill out the **Create Your Windows Live ID** form or click on the **File** tab, then click **Save & Send**. Click **Save to Web** and then click the **Sign Up for Windows Live** link.

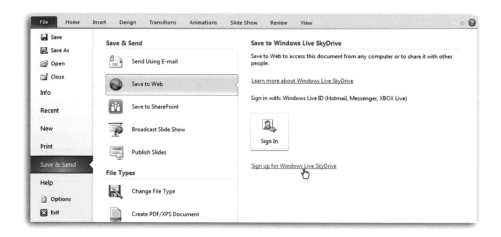

 What Microsoft Calls It: Broadcast a Slide Show

Step-by-Step

1. Open the presentation you want to broadcast, then click the **File** tab.

2. Click the **Save and Send** tab **A**, then select **Broadcast Slide Show** **B**.

3. In the right-most pane, click the **Broadcast Slide Show** button **C** to open the **Broadcast Slide Show** dialog box.

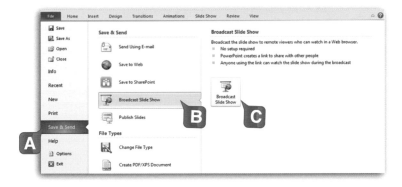

4. Click the **Change Broadcast Service** button **D** and select **PowerPoint Broadcast Service** **E**.

5. Click **Start Broadcast.** You will be prompted to sign in to your Windows Live account. Enter your username and password.

6. You will be given a link to share with the attendees of your presentation. Copy the link in the text box and send the URL to the other members. PowerPoint Broadcast Service can host up to 50 attendees.

   The attendees will see the message **Waiting for broadcast to begin** when they click on your link.

7. Click **Start Slide Show** F to start your presentation. Your attendees will see your first slide.

8. To finish your presentation, right-click and then choose **End** from the fly-out menu, or hit **Escape**.

Bright Idea: If you wish to narrate your presentation live, arrange a conference call for the attendees so they can hear you speak as you perform the slide show.

45 | Customize Your Presentation

Difficulty: ●●○○

PROBLEM You have created a comprehensive presentation to take with you on an upcoming sales trip. You will be giving presentations to several different customers and a handful of new leads. Your presentation contains all the information you need for all of the meetings, but you will not need every slide in every situation. You want a way to create different shows without creating a new presentation for each meeting.

SOLUTION Create a custom show. A custom show allows you to choose just the slides that you need for a specific audience.

See Also: Set Up Show

Step-by-Step

Create a Custom Show

1. Open the presentation you want to turn into a custom show, then click the **Slide Show** tab.

2. In the **Start Slide Show** group, click **Custom Slide Show** button **A**, then click **Custom Shows** to open the **Custom Shows** dialog box.

3. Click the **New** button **B** to open the **Define Custom Show** dialog box.

4. In the **Slides in presentation:** pane, click on the slide you want to include in the custom show. To select multiple slides in sequence, use **SHIFT+click**. To select multiple individual slides, use **CTRL+click**.

5. Click the **Add** button **C** to add the slides to the **Slides in custom show:** pane.

6. To reorder slides in the custom presentation, select the slide you want to move, then click the **Up** or **Down** buttons 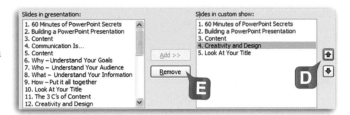 to move it to the position you want.

7. You can remove a slide from the custom presentation by selecting the slide and click the **Remove** button **E**.

8. Type a name for your custom show in the **Slide show name:** text box **F**. Be sure to choose a name that will identify the presentation so you will be able to find it quickly later.

9. Click **OK**. Repeat the above to create more custom shows from the same base presentation.

10. To set up your custom show, click the **Set Up Slide Show** button in the **Set Up** group on the **Slide Show** tab to launch the **Set Up Show** dialog box.

11. In the **Show slides** section, click the **Custom show:** radio button **G**, then select your custom show from the dropdown menu. Make any other setting choices you need, then click **OK**.

12. To play your custom show, click the **Custom Slide Show** button in the **Start Slide Show** group on the **Slide Show** tab, then click on the name of your custom show.

46 | Save a Presentation to Video

Difficulty: ●●○○

PROBLEM Rather than give a presentation to each new hire personally, the HR manager for your company has asked you to come up with a short video presentation to be shown at each new employee's orientation.

SOLUTION Save your presentation as a video. Within PowerPoint, you can choose to save your existing slide show as a video, enabling it to be shown multiple times, in high quality, and exactly the same way each time, without having to have someone manage the presentation each showing. When your presentation is in video format, your audience does not even have to have PowerPoint installed to watch your presentation.

Step-by-Step

1. Open the presentation you want to save as a video file. Remember, since you will not be present to introduce the material, enhance your presentation with audio and video content and record a narration to deliver your spoken message. *See also Create a Presentation to Run at a Kiosk; Record a Narration*

2. Check your presentation for media compatibility by clicking on the **Info** tab under the **File** tab. This tool will let you know if you have media files that will not work in your video. In this example, it shows that one media file requires a network connection **A** (a linked YouTube video) and, as such, will not be included the video. For best results, use embedded media to create a video.

3. Click the **File** tab, then click **Save & Send B**.

4. Under the **Save & Send** heading, click **Create a video C**.

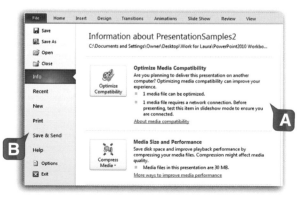

5. To choose the level of video quality for your presentation, click the **Computer & HD Displays** dropdown arrow and select an option from the menu:

- **Computer & HD Displays:** Highest quality and largest file size. Click this when you will be able to play the video directly from your own machine or from a corporate network drive.

- **Internet & DVD:** Medium quality video with moderate file sizes. Click this option for internet downloads and disk media delivery.

- **Portable Devices:** Lowest quality and file size. Click this option when your video will be viewed on portable devices such as Zunes or iPods, or when you will need to email copies of the video.

6. Click the **Use Recorded Timings and Narrations** dropdown arrow [E] and select an option from the menu:

- **Don't Use Recorded Timings and Narration:** Narrations and timings that you have already recorded into the presentation will not be used. Slides in the video will advance at the rate specified in the **Seconds to spend on each slide:** setting [F]. Click the up or down arrow to adjust this number.

- **Use Recorded Timings and Narrations:** Slides that contain narrations and timings will be played as set. Slides without a timing will advance at the rate specified in the **Seconds to spend on each slide:** setting.

CONTINUE▶

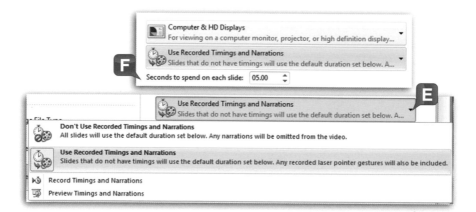

7. Click **Create Video** G. ⚠

8. Enter a name for your video in the **File name:** text box H.

9. Click **Save**.

Caution: Creating a video may take a long time, especially if the presentation is long and contains many animations, transitions, and embedded media. You can continue working in PowerPoint while the video is created, but you may want to start creating long videos when you can be away from your desk for a time, or overnight. You can monitor the progress of the video by looking at the status bar at the bottom of the screen .

47 | Create a PowerPoint Presentation from a Word Document

Difficulty: ●●●○

PROBLEM The head of the department just informed you that you need to create a PowerPoint presentation using the data from your monthly overview report and present it the executive team in three hours.

SOLUTION You can create a Microsoft PowerPoint presentation from an existing Word document. The Word document should be structured like an outline, using the predesigned heading styles in Word. PowerPoint uses these heading styles in the Word document to format the titles of each slide. For example, text formatted with the Heading 1 style becomes the title of a new slide. Text formatted with Heading 2 becomes the first level of text. This process will continue for all data formatted in this manner.

Step-by-Step

1. Create or open your outline in Word.

2. Select the text that will become a slide title and assign it as Heading 1 **A**.

3. Select each sub-heading text and assign it as Heading 2 **B**. Continue until all outline text is set.

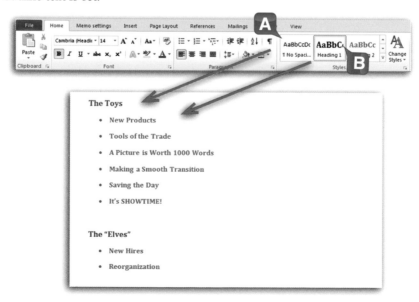

4. Save the Word document and close it.

5. Open **PowerPoint** and create a new presentation.

6. Add a new slide after the title slide.

7. On that new slide, click the dropdown arrow at the bottom of the **New Slide** combo button **C** and select **Slides from Outline D** to open the **Insert Outline** dialog box.

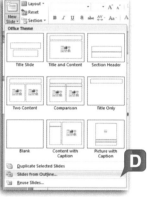

8. Browse to your Word file and select it.

9. Click the **Open** button.

Hot Tip: To save time formatting, decide what theme you want to use in the PowerPoint Slide Show. Use that same theme when you assign the heading styles to your outline in Word, as the selected style carries over into PowerPoint when you import the outline to the slides.

48 Reuse Slides in a Presentation

Difficulty: ●●○○

PROBLEM You are creating a presentation to show prospective buyers your company's latest product. Throughout the presentation, you want to compare your current product to the previous versions of the product. Rather than create new slides for the old product, you'd like to reuse slides that you've already made for an older presentation.

SOLUTION Reuse slides. The Reuse Slide feature allows you to browse through slides in older presentations and add them to your new presentation without having to leave the one you are working in.

Step-by-Step

1. Open the presentation you are working on.

2. In the **Slides** navigation pane, click between any two slides where you want the re-used slide to go.

3. Click the down arrow on the **New Slide** combo button  **A** to open the menu, then select **Reuse Slides** **B** to open the **Reuse Slides** task pane.

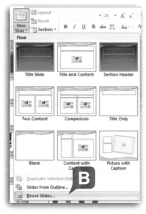

4. Click **Open a PowerPoint File** **C**, then browse to and select the file of the presentation that contains the slides you want to reuse in the **Browse** dialog box. Click **Open**. Thumbnails of the slides in the presentation you have selected will display in the **Reuse Slides** pane.

5. Click on a slide  **D** in the **Reuse Slide** pane to add it to your open presentation. To add all of the slides from the **Reuse Slide** pane, right-click, then select **Insert All Slides.**

The slides will be converted into the Theme style that you are using in the new presentation. To keep the Theme style of the original presentation, click the **Keep source formatting** checkbox **E** before you enter the slides. ⚠

Caution: Changing the theme of your source slides may introduce layout conflicts **F** in your new presentation. After you insert your slides from the **Reuse Slides** pane, make sure to check every one for problems.

49 | Customize the Quick Access Toolbar and Status Bar

Difficulty: ●●○○

PROBLEM There are several actions and commands you use frequently, but they are spread across multiple tabs and often several clicks deep. It would be helpful if they were available in one convenient menu.

SOLUTION The Quick Access Toolbar is a row of buttons in the top left corner of the PowerPoint window. This toolbar can be repositioned either above or below the Ribbon and can be customized. Buttons can be added, removed, or rearranged. The Status Bar is the bar at the bottom of the PowerPoint window. The status bar contains items such as page status, word count, page view buttons, and a zoom slide button.

Customizing the Quick Access Toolbar or the Status Bar allows you to quickly perform tasks that are not necessarily available through a shortcut key or available by clicking the Ribbon. Since utilizing this customization option is a highly individualized task, the variations are limitless.

Step-by-Step

1. Click the **Customize Quick Access Toolbar** button **A** to the right of the **Quick Access Toolbar**, at the top left corner of your window to open the dropdown menu.

2. If the command you want to add to the **Quick Access Toolbar** is on the default list of common commands, then click it. A checkmark will appear **B** by the command in the menu and the command's icon will appear **C** in the toolbar at the top of your window.

3. To choose from all available commands, click the **More Commands...** menu option **D** to open the **PowerPoint Options** dialog box.

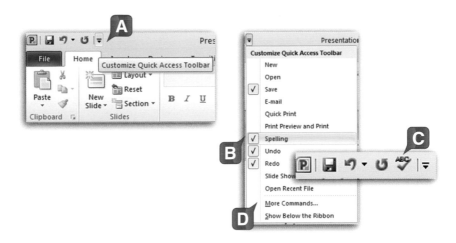

4. Open the **Choose commands from:** dropdown menu  and make a selection:

- **Popular commands:** This includes commands that PowerPoint users most frequently use in the Quick **Access Toolbar,** such as **Save**, **Open**, **New**, and **Print Preview**.

- **Commands not in the ribbon:** This includes features that were either available in a previous version of Word or only pertain to specific types of projects and are less frequently used. Microsoft did not put these commands on the 2010 ribbon.

- **All commands:** This includes a list of all available commands.

- **Macros:** This includes a list of all available macros.

- You can also choose from commands as they are organized on the ribbon. Click the **Drawing Tools | Format Tab** option **F**, for example, to see all the commands that are visible only when an image or photograph is selected.

5. Select a command from the left pane, then click **Add** . The command will be added to the **Quick Access Toolbar** pane with your existing choices. Add more commands as desired.

6. To arrange the order you would like the commands to appear, click on the **Up/ Down** arrows **H** to the right of the toolbar pane to move the commands up and down (right or left in your toolbar).

7. Click on the **Customize Quick Access Toolbar:** dropdown **I** to choose whether you wish these settings to apply to all presentations you open in PowerPoint, or only for the document you are currently working on.

8. Click **OK**. Your new commands will appear in your **Quick Access Toolbar**.

Step-by-Step

Customize the Status Bar

1. Right-click the **Status Bar** **J**.

2. A menu opens with check marks next to the displayed items **K**. Click an item to toggle it on or off.

3. Checked items will be active and visible on the status bar.

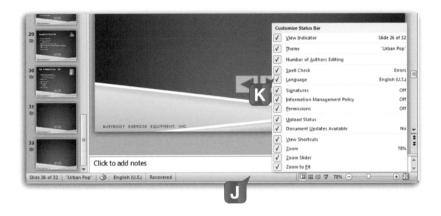

50 Use Find and Replace

Difficulty: ●●○○

PROBLEM You realize that you need to change text in your presentation. You have spelled the name "Ann" (one of your customers) incorrectly throughout your presentation, and you need to replace her name with the correct spelling, "Anne." Editing the presentation text manually could cause a missed case of the error and is very time-consuming.

SOLUTION The Find feature helps locate instances of a specified string of text. It can also locate specific formatting, or a non-printing symbol or code. The Replace feature then takes the next step of replacing the found item with a different text string. There are a variety of useful functions in the Editing tool.

Step-by-Step

1. On the **Home** tab in the **Editing** group, click **Find** **A** to open the **Find** dialog box.

2. Type the text string you are looking for into the **Find what:** text box **B** and hit **Find Next**.

3. PowerPoint will highlight matches for your search in the current page on the document pane **C**. Click **Find Next** to navigate to the next occurrence of the phrase or word.

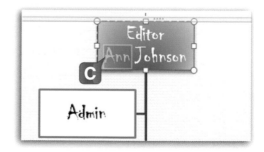

4. To replace your search phrase with new text, click the **Replace** button in the **Editing** group on the **Home** tab to open the **Replace** dialog box. Enter the correct text in the **Replace with:** text box .

Click the **Match case** or **Find whole words only** checkboxes if you want PowerPoint to only return results that match case as well as spelling ("Word" vs. "word") or to prevent results that include your text string within another word ("and" vs. "android").

5. Click **Replace**. PowerPoint will highlight the next match it finds. Click **Replace** again to make the change or **Find Next** to skip that match. Click **Replace All** to allow PowerPoint to replace all matches without reviewing each change.

6. Repeat until PowerPoint has finished searching the presentation.

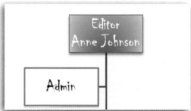

Caution: Replace All is a quick way to substitute text throughout the entire document. However, you must be careful that the string of text does not exist as a part of any other words in the document. For example, you are using the **Find and Replace** function to replace the misspelled name "Ann" with "Anne". If you have the word "Annuity" in your document, the **Replace All** function will change your word to "Anneuity". To correct for this, make sure you choose to replace "Ann" (with a space after the second "n") with "Anne" (with a space after the "e"). This will allow you to make the replacement without introducing additional errors.

51 | Use Slide Masters

Difficulty: ●●○○

PROBLEM You want to have a way to make a configuration change across all the slides in your presentation instead of making the same edits on each slide of a long presentation. Furthermore, you have three distinct sections of your presentation that you want to reflect with distinct changes in theme and font choices, but you don't want to edit every slide as you go.

SOLUTION Use a Slide Master. A Slide Master is the top slide on the list of master slides that stores information about the theme, layout and positions of items on the slides, and information such as colors used in the presentation. Using a Slide Master, you can make style changes to every slide in your presentation at the same time, as well as have those changes apply to any new slides that you might add dialog box.

Step-by-Step

---

Edit a Slide Master

1. Open the presentation you want to make changes to, then click the **View** tab.

2. In the **Master Views** group, click the **Slide Master** button **A** to open the **Slide Master** tab. The **Slide Master** is the larger slide image in the thumbnail pane **B**. Layouts associated with that master are listed underneath **C**.

3. Edit the title style and text styles by clicking in the textboxes and selecting your new settings from the **Edit Theme** group **D**.

Change the way the background looks by selecting options in the **Background Styles** menu **E** in the **Background** group.

Set the page orientation of your slides by selecting options in the **Page Setup** group **F**.

Right-click on the text or objects for more formatting options, such as bullet style **G** and text effects **H**.

Adjust and customize date and footer text **I**.

Changes you make on the Master Slide will affect all layout slides below it. *See also: Create and Save Custom Layouts*

CONTINUE

4. When your Master Slide looks how you want it, click the **File** tab, then click **Save As**  to open the **Save As** dialog box.

5. Type a name for your **Master Slide** design in the **File name:** text box **K**.

6. In the **Save as type** dropdown list, choose **PowerPoint Template** **L**, and then click **Save**.

7. Click the **Close Master View** button to close the **Slide Master** tab and return to editing your presentation.

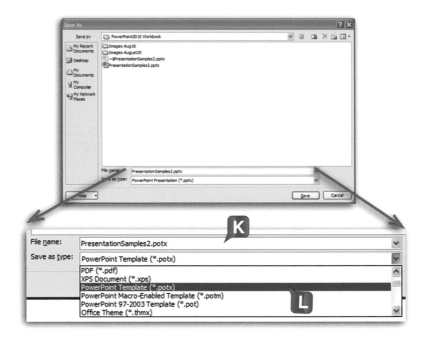

 **Step-by-Step**

Add Multiple Themes to Your Presentation

For a presentation to use multiple themes, you will need to add a **Slide Master** and layout slides for each theme you want represented.

1. Open the **Slide Master** tab by clicking the **Slide Master** button in the **View** tab.

2. Scroll to the bottom of the slides thumbnail list and click in the space just below the last slide. A blinking black line will appear.

3. Click the **Themes** button **M** in the **Edit Theme** group to open the **Themes** menu.

4. Click on the theme that most closely meets your needs. A **Slide Master** for that theme and a default set of layout slides will be added to the thumbnail list **N**.

5. Click the **Close Master View** button to close the **Slide Master** tab and return to editing your presentation. The slide layouts for the theme you just added will now be available under the **New Slide** button on the **Home** tab **O**.

See also: Create a Custom Theme; Create and Save Custom Layouts

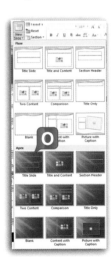

52 Edit Handouts and Notes Masters

Difficulty: ●●○○

PROBLEM You are in charge of making handouts for all the students in your class and you would like to add text to every handout with the lesson number, title, and date in the headers and footers. You would also like to add a text box that prompts students to write down the reading homework associated with each slide's topic.

SOLUTION Much like a Slide Master, you may also have a Master for your Handouts and Notes as well. Changes made to the Notes or Handout Masters will be reflected on each Handout or Note, simply by changing and saving the Master.

Step-by-Step

1. Open the presentation your handouts will come from, then click the **View** tab.

2. In the **Master Views** group, click the **Handout Master** button **A** to open the **Handout Master** tab.

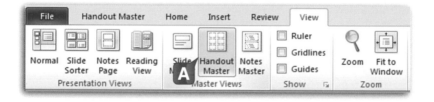

3. In the **Page Setup** group, make selections and adjustments to prepare the handouts the way you want them to print.

   - **Page Setup:** Click to set page height and width and choose slide numbering options **B**.
   - **Handout Orientation:** Click to choose print page orientation **C**.
   - **Slide Orientation:** Click to choose orientation of slides on the handout **D**.
   - **Slides Per Page:** Click to choose the number of slides that will be shown per printed page **E**.

4. In the **Placeholders** group **F**, check the elements you want printed on your handouts.

5. Type any text you want to appear in the **Header** and **Footer**. This text will appear only on handouts.

6. In the **Background** group, click the **Background Styles** dropdown menu to choose a style for your handouts. These changes do not affect your slides or notes. ⚠

7. When you have made all the adjustments you need, click the **Close Master View** button **G**.

8. Print your handouts. *See also: Create Handouts*

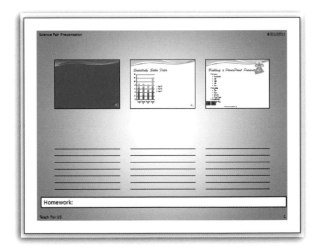

53 Proof Your Presentation with Spell Check and Thesaurus Tools

Difficulty: ●●○○

PROBLEM Rather than viewing each slide individually to check for misspellings and grammatical errors, as well as to make sure that you have varied your language in order to keep the audience's attention, you would prefer a way within PowerPoint to help you find and correct errors.

SOLUTION PowerPoint, like other Microsoft Office products, features a range of Spelling and Thesaurus options. From choosing to allow PowerPoint to auto-correct your text to manually prompting PowerPoint to check each slide individually, options can be turned on and off based on the user's preferences.

Step-by-Step

Check for Spelling Errors

1. Click the **Review** tab, then click the **Spelling** button **A** in the **Proofing** group.

2. If any spelling errors are found, the **Spelling** dialog box will open and the word in question will appear in the **Not in Dictionary:** text box **B**. The slide that contains the error will open and the misspelled word will be highlighted **C**.

3. When PowerPoint finds a word it does not recognize, you have several options to resolve the error:

- Type the correct word into the **Change to:** text box **D** manually and then click the **Change** button **E**. Click the **Change All** button **F** to make this correction *every* time this word appears in your presentation.

- Select a word from the **Suggestions:** list **G** and then click the **Change** button to use a suggested word. Click the **Change All** button **F** to make this correction *every* time this word appears in your presentation.

- Click the **Ignore** button **H** to leave the word alone this time. Click the **Ignore All** button **I** to leave the word as it is every time it appears in this presentation.

- Click the **Add** button **J** to add the word to Microsoft Office's Dictionary ⚠.

- If you make this same mistake often and would like Office to replace the word with the correct spelling *every* time you type the mistake version of the word, type the correct spelling in the **Change to:** text box, then click the **AutoCorrect** button **K**.

4. When you have made your selection, the spell checker will advance to the next incorrect word until all unrecognized words have been addressed.

Step-by-Step

Use the Thesaurus

1. Select the word you want to look up in the Thesaurus, then click the **Review** tab.

2. Click the **Thesaurus** button  to open the **Research** pane.

3. The word you have selected will be in the **Search for:** text box **M** and the **English (U.S.) Thesaurus** will be pre-selected in the **Research Options** dropdown list **N**.

4. To replace your word with one of the words that the Thesaurus returns, click on it, then click on the dropdown arrow that appears.

5. Click **Insert** **O**. The new word will appear in your slide. If you need synonyms for other words, type them into the **Search for:** text box, then click the **Start Searching** button **P**.

6. Close the **Research** pane when you are finished by clicking the **Close** button **Q**.

Caution: When you add a word to the Microsoft Office Dictionary, it will be used by *all* Office programs that offer Spell Check. Make sure the words you add will be correct in most contexts that you will use them.

54 | Research a Topic

Difficulty: ●●○○

PROBLEM You are preparing a presentation for your economics class and you want to include current statistics to illustrate the concepts you are demonstrating. You'd like a quick way to look up the numbers without having to leave your browser before you leave your presentation.

SOLUTION Use the Research pane. The PowerPoint research pane gives you access to reference books and research sites from within the PowerPoint window. In addition to several language resources, you can also search business and financial sites or the Bing™ search engine.

Step-by-Step

1. Click the **Research** button **A** on the **Review** tab to open the **Research** pane.

2. Enter a search phrase for the information you are looking for in the **Search for:** text box **B**.

3. Click the down arrow in the **Research Options** list **C**. Select the reference book or web site you want to search within.

4. Click the **Start Searching** button **D**. Your results will display in the results window **E**.

5. Click on the result that best matches your query. If the resource is a website, a browser window will open in your default web browser to display the complete article. If the result is a translation or thesarus result, click on it to open more options.

Bright Idea: If there are research services that you use regularly and would like to access from the **Research** pane, add them to the **Research Options** list by clicking **Research Options...** at the bottom of the pane, then **Add**

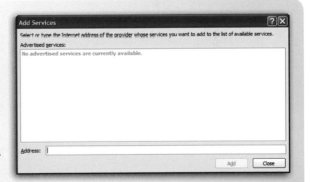

Services... to open the **Add Services** dialog box. Type the URL of the service into the **Address:** text box, then click **Add**.

55 | PowerPoint Translation Tools

Difficulty: ●●○○

PROBLEM You are creating a presentation that will be shown not only to sales agents within your home country, but those in the field offices of other countries and territories as well, encompassing a wide range of different languages.

SOLUTION PowerPoint contains built-in dictionaries for many of the most common languages spoken across the world. You can access these dictionaries and translation tools through the Review menu and can translate one slide at a time into an available language, or you can translate a presentation in a language unfamiliar to you into your home language.

Step-by-Step

Translate Selected Text

1. Select the word or phrase you want to translate, then click the **Review** tab.

2. Click the **Research** button  to open the **Research** pane. The word or phrase will appear in the **Search for:** text box **B**.

3. Select **Translation C** from the **Research Options** dropdown list.

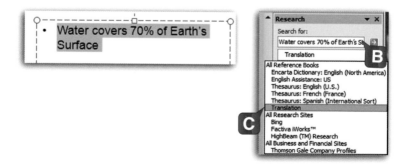

4. Select the languages you are translating **From**  and **To** E in the dropdown lists. Your translation results will appear under the **Microsoft Translator** heading F. ✻

5. To replace your selected text with the translation, click the **Insert** button G. ⚠

Step-by-Step

Use the Mini Translator

Introduced in Office 2010, the Microsoft Mini Translator allows you to select words or phrases and see a translation of those words in a small, pop-up window. Use this when you receive documents or e-mail that contain words in another language that you are unsure of.

1. To turn the Mini-Translator on, open the **Review** tab, then click the **Translate** button H in the **Language** group.

2. Click **Mini Translator** I to open the **Translation Language Options** dialog box.

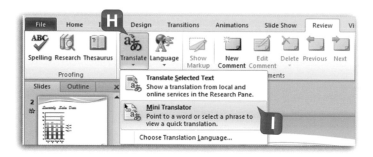

3. Select the language you want the **Mini Translator** to translate into from the **Translate to:** dropdown list **J**.

4. Click **OK** to turn on **Mini Translator.** When you hover over words or select phrases, a ghosted pane will pop up behind your cursor. Mouse over the pop-up pane to view the translation **K**.

5. The **Mini Translator** will remain on until you turn it off by repeating steps 1-2 above.

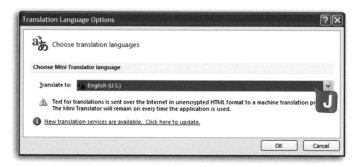

Quickest Click: Select a word or phrase and then, right-click. Choose **Translate**  from the fly-out menu to open the **Research** pane. The phrase will appear in the **Search for:** text box and the **Research Options** dropdown list will be set to the **Translation** options.

Caution: Machine translation should only be used to help understand or convey basic subject matter. For accurate translations, especially if important business or legal communication is needed, it is always best to have translations approved by a native speaker or translation specialist.

56 | Leave Comments on a Slide

Difficulty: ●●○○

PROBLEM You are creating a seating chart for your classroom using PowerPoint. You want to add notes on each individual student next to the desk where they will be assigned. As these notes are for the teacher, you do not want them to appear on any handouts of the seating chart that are made.

SOLUTION PowerPoint comments work in a similar way to those in Microsoft Word. You can insert a comment at any place on a slide, and each comment that is added will include the initials of the person who wrote it as well as the comment number. Hovering the mouse pointer over a comment or double-clicking on it will open a window to show the comments.

 ## Step-by-Step

Create a Comment

1. Select the object or text that you want to associate with a comment. If you want to add a general comment about the slide as a whole, click anywhere on the slide. Click the **Review** tab.

2. Click the **New Comment** button **A** in the **Comments** group.

3. Type your comments in the comment box **B** that appears next to your object. The comment will be tagged with the user name associated with your copy of PowerPoint **C** and stamped with the date **D**.

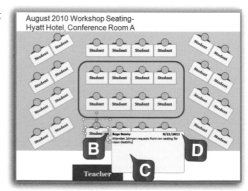

4. To review comments, click on the comment thumbnail, then click the **Edit Comment** button **E** in the **Comments** group.

5. Make your changes in the comment box. If you are editing a comment written by another reviewer, the color of the thumbnail will change and your initials will replace that of the initial reviewer.

6. To delete comments, click the **Delete F** button and select a delete option from the menu:
   • **Delete** will delete only the comment you have selected.
   • **Delete All Markup on the Current Slide** will remove all comments on the slide you are currently editing.
   • **Delete All Markup in the Presentation** will remove all comments from your entire PowerPoint presentation. ✹

Hot Tip: To quickly move between comments in a presentation, click the **Previous** and **Next** buttons **G**.

If you do not see your comment thumbnails on the **Review** tab, check to see that the **Show Markup** button **H** is selected.

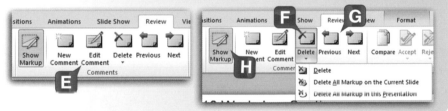

Quickest Click: To edit, copy, delete, or add a new comment to the same object, right-click a comment thumbnail and choose from the fly-out menu.
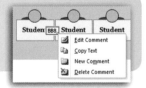

Bright Idea: Leave audio comments for your slides by recording your message with the **Record Audio** option in the **Media** group on the **Insert** tab.

57 | Compare and Combine Presentations

Difficulty: ●●○○

PROBLEM Two separate presentations have been made for the upcoming investor's meeting. You have been asked to look at them both and decide which will be presented. You would like an easy way to compare the two presentations and, if necessary, combine them into a single slideshow.

SOLUTION You can view two presentations at the same time by opening both slideshows, choosing View on the Ribbon, and selecting Arrange all. Using the Insert command, you can select a slide in a presentation, and then choose slides from another presentation to copy into the original. The new slides will be added after the slide that you have chosen on the original presentation.

Step-by-Step

Compare Presentations

1. Open the original presentation (or the first of the two), then click the **Review** tab.

2. Click the **Compare** button **A** in the **Compare** group to open the **Choose File to Merge with Current Presentation** dialog box.

3. Browse for the edited presentation (or second of the two) you want to compare and select it. Click **Merge**.

4. The **Reviewing** pane **B** will open to show differences between the versions and a thumbnail will appear by each change in the slides. Move between the revisions with the **Previous C** and **Next D** buttons.

5. When a change is highlighted, the **Accept** button **E** will become active. Click the down arrow to select from the menu options:

   • **Accept Change** – Approve this change only and apply the change to the merged document.

   • **Accept All Changes to the Current Slide** – Approve all the changes made to the slide you are viewing and apply the changes to the merged document.

   • **Accept All Changes to the Presentation** – Approve all the changes made to the entire presentation and apply the changes to the merged document.

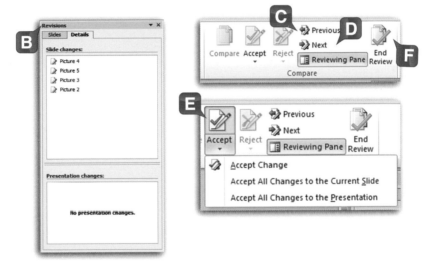

6. When you finish reviewing all the changes, click the **End Review** button **F**. Click **Yes** when prompted.

7. Save your updated presentation by clicking the **File** tab and then clicking the **Save As** button. Give your new file a new name to preserve all versions in the document's history.

58 | Slide Libraries

Difficulty: ●●○○

PROBLEM Your department creates many PowerPoint presentations over the course of a sales cycle. Your projects tend to be consistent, and it would save time to reuse or adapt slides already created for similar presentations. You would like a way to view all the slides that you have made using Microsoft PowerPoint in a single location, regardless of the date that those slides were made, or which of the presentations they were originally within.

SOLUTION With an optional program, Office SharePoint Server, you can set up a storage file that will contain all the slides that you and any others who have access to the storage server have made with Microsoft PowerPoint. These slides will be available for downloading and sharing in the workplace.

Step-by-Step

Add Slides to a Slide Library

1. Open the presentation that contains the slides you want to save to the **Slide Library**, then click the **File** tab.

2. Click **Save & Send** , then **Publish Slides** **B**. Click the **Publish Slides** button **C** in the rightmost pane to open the **Publish Slides** dialog box.

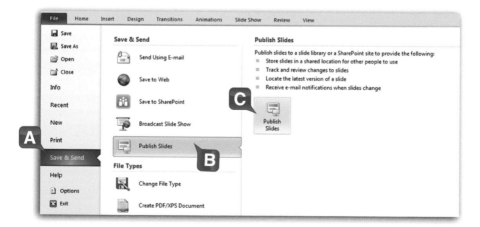

3. Click the checkboxes next to each slide that you want to add to the **Slide Library**. To select all slides in the presentation, click the **Select All** button.

4. To give the slides unique file names (instead of the presentation's default slide file names), click on the file name, then type in your new text.

5. Click in the description column to add a text description of the slide.

6. When your slides are selected and edited to your satisfaction, click on, or enter the URL for, the location of your **Slide Library** in the **Publish To:** dialog box.

7. Click the **Publish** button.

Step-by-Step

Use Slides from a Slide Library in Your Presentation

1. Click the down arrow on the **New Slide** combo button  in the **Slides** group on the **Home** tab to open the dropdown menu.

2. Click **Reuse Slides**  to open the **Reuse Slides** task pane.

3. Click the **Open a Slide Library** link **F** in the **Reuse Slides** task pane to open the **Select a Slide Library** dialog box.

4. Browse to the location of the **Slide Library** you want to use, then click **Select** to open the **Slide Library**.

5. Click the slide that you want to add to your presentation from the **All Slides** list.

A | Save a Presentation to the Appropriate File Format

Step-by-Step

Choose a File Format When Saving a Presentation

1. Click on the **File** tab.

2. Click **Save As** **A** to open the **Save As** dialog box.

3. Type in a file name for your presentation in the **File name:** text box **B**.

4. Select a file type from the **Save as type:** dropdown menu **C**:

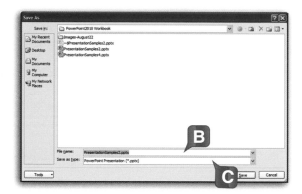

- **PowerPoint Presentation:** .PPTX The default format for PowerPoint 2010.

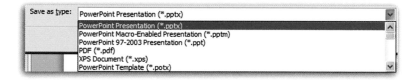

- **PowerPoint Macro-Enabled Presentation:** .PPTM This format is essentially the same as the default format, except that it can store macros. If you include macros, you will be prompted to save in this format. The .POTM format, PowerPoint Macro-Enabled Design Template is also available.

- **PowerPoint 97-2003 Presentation:** .PPT This is a format fully accessible by previous versions of PowerPoint back to 97. The .POT format, 97-2003 template, is also available.

- **PowerPoint Template:** .POTX The PowerPoint 2010 format for templates.
- **PDF and XPS:** .PDF and .XPS are read-only formats that will produce easy to read, share, and print documents. Open the **Options** dialog box for more .PDF settings.

- **GIF Graphic Interchange Format:** Converts each slide in your PowerPoint presentation into a picture in a GIF format.
- **JPEG:** Converts each slide in your PowerPoint presentation into a picture in a JPEG format. This is a smaller file than the GIF format.
- **PNG Portable Network Graphic Format:** Converts each slide in your PowerPoint presentation into a picture in the PNG format. This is a larger file and higher quality photo than either JPEG or GIF.
- **TIFF Tag Image File Format:** Converts each slide in your PowerPoint presentation into a picture in the TIFF format. This is the same quality as a PNG format.
- **Outline/RTF:** .RTF Converts PowerPoint Presentation into a text document in the form of an outline.

5. Click the **Save** button.

B | Customize Your PowerPoint Environment

Step-by-Step

Set User Preferences in PowerPoint

1. Click the **File** tab.

2. Click the **Options** button 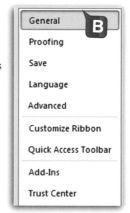 to launch the **PowerPoint Options** dialog box.

3. Click the menu tabs to view the options you want to adjust 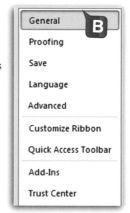.

- **General:** Change some basic defaults within PowerPoint, including User Interface Options, and Personalize Your Copy of Microsoft Office.

- **Proofing:** Modify how PowerPoint corrects and formats text. AutoCorrect, Spelling in Microsoft Programs; and Spelling in PowerPoint preferences are set here.

- **Save:** Customize how presentations are saved and how AutoRecover information is handled.

- **Language:** Choose your Office language preferences for proofing (spelling, grammar, etc.) and Help texts.

- **Advanced:** Modify many additional PowerPoint settings, including Cut/Copy/ Paste preferences, Image handling, and Editing preferences. Note that many of the settings adjusted here have ramifications that should be carefully considered before changes are made.

- **Customize Ribbon:** Add/remove or regroup items on the **Ribbon**.

- **Quick Access Toolbar:** Add/remove items to/from the **Quick Access Toolbar.**

- **Add-Ins:** Manage your PowerPoint **Add-Ins**. Note that most installed **Add-Ins** will not appear on the **Add-Ins** tab unless they are active.

- **Trust Center:** Manage document security settings.

4. Click the **OK** button.

Customize the Ribbon

Office 2010 introduced the ability to customize ribbon commands to a much greater degree. In 2010, you can create custom tabs and groups, rename and change the order of default tabs and groups, and hide both custom and default tabs.

To access the Customize options, click on the **File** tab, then click the **Options** button. This will launch the **PowerPoint Options** dialog box. Click on the **Customize Ribbon** tab .

Step-by-Step

Customize Tabs

1. To add a new tab to the **Ribbon**, click the **New Tab** button **B** under the **Customize the Ribbon:** window in the **PowerPoint Options** dialog box. A new tab with the name **New Tab (Custom)** **C** will appear in the list. ✻

2. Select the new tab and click the **Rename** button **D**.Type your custom tab name in the **Rename** dialog box **E**.

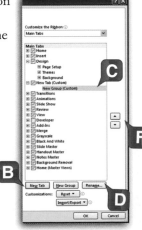

3. Click the **OK** button.

4. To move your new tab up and down on the list (or right and left on the **Ribbon**), select it, then click the up/down arrows to the right of the window **F**.

5. To hide a tab from being displayed on the ribbon, click the checkbox to the left of each tab **G** to uncheck it. Click again to unhide the tab and have it displayed in the **Ribbon**.

6. If you decide to remove a custom tab, right-click the tab in the **Customize the Ribbon:** list, then select **Remove H**. *Note:* You can hide, but you cannot remove default tabs.

Step-by-Step

Customize Groups

1. Click the **Expand** button **I** to the right of any tab to view the groups that appear on the tab.

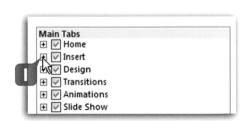

2. To add a new group to any tab, select the tab you want the group to appear on, then click the **New Group** button **J** under the **Customize the Ribbon:** window. A new group with the name **New Group (Custom) K** will appear in the list.

3. Right-click on the new group and select the **Rename** menu option **L** to open the **Rename** dialog box.

4. Type your custom group name in the **Display name:** text box **M**. You can also select an icon to represent your custom group by clicking on any image in the **Symbol:** selection box **N**.

5. Click the **OK** button.

6. To move your new group up and down on the list (or right and left on the tab), select it, then click the up/down arrows to the right of the **Customize the Ribbon:** list.

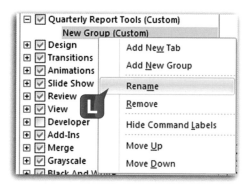

7. If you decide to remove a group from a tab, right-click the group in the **Customize the Ribbon:** list, then select **Remove** – OR – select the group, then click the **Remove** button **O** between the **Choose** and **Customize** windows.

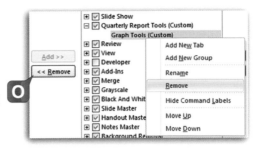

Step-by-Step

Add Commands to a Custom Group

1. Commands can only be added to custom groups, so begin by following the steps in the *Customize Groups* section to create a group for your commands.

2. Click on the command you want to add **P** in the **Choose commands from:** window.

3. Click on the destination custom group **Q**.

4. Click the **Add** button **R**. Repeat as needed.

5. The command will appear under your custom group in the **Customize the Ribbon:** list.

6. To rename a command that you have added to a custom group, right-click on the command and select the **Rename** menu option. Type your command name in the **Rename** dialog box. You can also select an icon to represent your custom group by clicking on any image in the **Symbol:** selection box.

7. To move a command up and down on the list, select it, then click the up/down arrows to the right of the window.

8. If you decide to remove a command from your custom group, right-click the group in the **Customize the Ribbon:** list, then select **Remove** – OR – select the group, then click the **Remove** button between the **Choose** and **Customize** windows.

    Note: You cannot remove commands from default groups, although you can remove entire groups from tabs. *See Also: Customize Groups*

9. When you have made all your changes, click **OK** in the **PowerPoint Options** dialog box to save your settings and return to your presentation. Review your customized tab.

Quickest Click: Right-click any item in the **Customize the Ribbon:** window for shortcuts to add new tabs or groups, show or hide tabs, and move tabs up or down.

D Keyboard Shortcuts

Keyboard Shortcut	Description
Common Tasks	
CTRL+SHIFT+SPACEBAR	Create a nonbreaking space
CTRL+SHIFT+HYPHEN	Create a nonbreaking hyphen
CTRL+B	Bold text
CTRL+I	Italic text
CTRL+U	Underline text
CTRL+SHIFT+<	Shrink font size one increment
CTRL+SHIFT+>	Grow font size one increment
CTRL+A	Select All (effect depends on the tab you are working in)
CTRL+C	Copy selected text or object
CTRL+X	Cut selected text or object to the Office Clipboard
CTRL+V	Paste text or an object
CTRL+ALT+V	Paste special
CTRL+SHIFT+V	Paste formatting only
CTRL+Z	Undo the last action
CTRL+Y	Redo the last action
CTRL+K	Insert hyperlink
Document Shortcuts	
CTRL+N	Create a new presentation
CTRL+O	Open a presentation
CTRL+W	Close a presentation window
CTRL+S	Save a presentation
CTRL+P	Print a presentation
ALT+CTRL+M	Insert a comment
CTRL+F6	Switch to next PowerPoint window

Editing Shortcuts Note: Cursor needs to be inside a text box for these shortcuts	
BACKSPACE	Delete one character to the left
CTRL+BACKSPACE	Delete one word to the left
DELETE	Delete one character to the right
CTRL+DELETE	Delete one word to the right
CTRL+SHIFT+F	Change font
CTRL+SHIFT+P	Change font size
SHIFT+RIGHT ARROW	Select one character to the right
SHIFT+LEFT ARROW	Select one character to the left
CTRL+SHIFT+RIGHT ARROW	Select to the end of a word
CTRL+SHIFT+LEFT ARROW	Select to the beginning of a word
CTRL+A	Select all objects in a presentation
CTRL+E	Center paragraph
CTRL+J	Justify paragraph
CTRL+L	Left align paragraph
CTRL+R	Right align paragraph
CTRL+SPACEBAR	Remove paragraph or character formatting

Slide Show Shortcuts (must be in SlideShow View to use these shortcuts)	
N, ENTER, PAGE DOWN, RIGHT ARROW, DOWN ARROW, or SPACEBAR	Advance – Perform the next animation or move to the next slide
P, PAGE UP, LEFT ARROW, UP ARROW, or BACKSPACE	Previous – Perform the previous animation or return to the previous slide
number+ENTER	Jump to a specific slide number
B ; PERIOD	Show a blank, black slide; Return from a blank, black slide
W ; COMMA	Show a blank, white slide; Return from a blank, white slide

S	Stop or restart a self-running presentation
ESC or HYPHEN	End presentation
A or =	Show/Hide arrow pointer
CTRL+P	Change pointer into pen
CTRL+A	Change pointer into arrow
CTRL+E	Change pointer into eraser
CTRL+H	Hide pointer and navigation button
CTRL+S	View All Slides dialog box
ALT+Q	Stop media playback during presentation
ALT+P	Play/Pause toggle
ALT+END	Go to next bookmark
ALT+HOME	Go to previous bookmark
ALT+UP	Increase media volume
ALT+DOWN	Decrease media volume
ALT+U	Mute volume
Function Keys	
F1	Open Help or visit Microsoft Office.com
F2	Rename
F4	Save As
F5	Start Slide Show from beginning
F6	Go to the next pane or frame
F7	Choose the Spelling command (Review tab)
F10	Show KeyTips (see also: "The Magic ALT Key")

The "Magic" ALT Key

When you press the ALT key on your keyboard, letters appear on the ribbon. Clicking a letter launches the corresponding function. Unlike other keyboard shortcuts, ALT shortcut keys are pressed sequentially, not held down at once. This can be much faster than using the mouse.

Index